3

To Carl Hoffman —
Long-time partner in
our exciting adventure of
building Mc Kinsey &
Company into a world
wide force for strength-
ening the will to
manage.

With warm regards,

Marvin B

15 Oct 66

The Will to Manage

Corporate Success through Programmed Management

MARVIN BOWER

Managing Director, McKinsey & Company, Inc.

McGRAW-HILL BOOK COMPANY

New York   San Francisco   Toronto   London   Sydney

The What, Why, and for Whom of This Book

Once upon a time, but not many years ago, there was a very able young manager who was promoted to general manager of a very large division of a very large corporation. Unfortunately, the profits of this division were very unsatisfactory. For the products it made were very much like the products of all its competitors, and the capacity of the industry was very much larger than the demand.

When he found out the predicament he was in, the very able young manager—who had always been very successful—became very unhappy. So the very able young manager decided he must *do* something. But he did not know *what* to do. Having been promoted from a division that made a very different kind of product, he was new to the business. So he arranged for his 15 top managers to spend two days at a nearby motel examining their predicament in depth. "Don't bother to bring figures," he told them. "I want you to *think*—and I want you to think mostly about *customers* and *markets* and what goes on *outside* the business."

The two-day meeting was not very productive. Because the business had been run without concept, principle, or philosophy to guide it, the 15 top managers had not been used to thinking very much. Instead, they had been very busy preparing and studying masses of figures, jockeying to strengthen their personal positions, and shaving prices to keep the plants going and to meet competition. In other words, they had been engaging in *ad hoc,* piecemeal, day-to-day, personal power management.

However, the very able young manager was not discouraged. Two weeks later he took his 15 top managers to another motel for another two-day meeting—and again he required them to think deeply about the business, especially about customers, markets, and forces at work outside the business. In this second session they began to get ideas—and in subsequent sessions, real results. They rediscovered simple, traditional managing processes. They took actions and made decisions that now began to seem very obvious. They began to face up to things they had really known about all along but had not done enough about in a systematic, consistent fashion.

The very able young manager inspired and required his 15 top managers to do these very obvious things very well and very consistently, as part of a comprehensive over-all program or system. And this they did—under his insistent leadership—because the very able young manager had a very strong *will to manage.*

Within a year the profits of the division were very much higher—in fact, they were 70 percent higher. Then the very able young manager was no longer perplexed; in fact, he was very happy. And the top management of his company was happier still. Then, after a few more years of outstanding performance, the very able young manager was promoted again.

Moral: The key to corporate success is a leader with a strong will to manage, who inspires and requires able people to work purposefully and effectively through simple and traditional managing processes that are integrated into a management program or system tailored to the nature and environment of the business.

That moral is the theme of this book. For the story of the able young manager is *not* a fable. It is the true story of a Midwestern business success. From that story, and from the actual experiences of many other able managers, I have tried to distill insights to show how simple, fundamental, and well-known managing processes can be systematically applied to achieve greater business success. In short, this is a nontechnical (and, I hope, readable) book about managing a business successfully.

In it, I am primarily concerned with success-proven principles for applying existing knowledge, not with creating new knowledge. The managing processes I discuss are not new. Nor are the ways of using them. I make no apology for dealing with these fundamentals, however, because it is from them that a system for successful management can best be fashioned.

The importance of the *will to manage*, however, is not yet widely recognized. Although systematized management is a recent but fairly well established concept, it is not fully understood or consciously practiced in a great many companies. Still less appreciated is the value of the management system in effectively implementing management will.

My thesis is not simply that managers should learn how to use established management know-how better before they try new techniques. Rather, I am arguing that management methods—new *and* old—will be more effective when they are held together with the glue of principle and fitted into a system that gives added leverage to each. And systematized management will enable any company to keep in better step with the vast technological, social, and political changes that are part of the business environment.

I focus on those aspects of managing where I believe I have

gained valuable insights from firsthand observation and analysis of successful company experience—experience that I illustrate with case examples.

Since I have written this book chiefly out of my own experience as a management consultant, some account of that experience is in order. So let me describe it briefly and thereafter keep in the background, where every author belongs unless he is writing an autobiography.

Over the years I have worked with small teams of consultants on the top-management problems of successful companies in a wide range of industries. The majority of these companies have been both large and successful. Most of those I have worked with during the past 15 years have been unquestioned leaders in their industries—first, second, or third in volume and profits.

The job of a team of management consultants is to develop, and to persuade client executives to adopt, improvements in company objectives, strategy, policies, organization structure, and management methods that will strengthen their competitive position, increase their profits, and help ensure continuity of effective management.

In doing so, we analyze the economics of the business and the environment in which it operates. We learn the company's competitive strengths and weaknesses and the philosophy of management that made it successful. We gather facts inside and outside the company. We observe and analyze management processes at close range. We discuss, in confidence, the successes as well as the mistakes of the company and of individual managers. We explore the workability of various possibilities for solving problems and improving performance.

All management consultants have an unusual management-methods laboratory, dealing as we do with live management problems and opportunities in a broad cross section of business and government organizations. In this respect I have been unusually fortunate. In more than 30 years as a management consultant, I have spent a good deal of time behind the scenes of many large, successful corporations in the U.S. and Europe. And since my own career has roughly coincided with the rise of the management consulting profession, not many others have had comparable opportunities to observe and analyze at firsthand how large and successful companies are managed.

Believing as I do that every American has a duty to do what he can to help increase the strength, productivity, and character-building contributions of our private-enterprise system, I feel some obligation to make the distillate of my experience available to others.

In addition to my own consulting experience, I have drawn on that of my colleagues, principally in order to check my own views on critical issues. Some of them differ with me on quite a few points, which is not surprising, since McKinsey & Company does not believe in standardized approaches or ready-made solutions. In the last analysis, therefore, the ideas and recommendations in this book are mine alone.

Since most of the material has been gathered in the course of my professional work, many outstanding client managers have contributed to this book without intending to do so. Even though the successful executive is usually quite willing to share his experience with others, it would hardly be appropriate to identify these men, or in most instances their companies, without their approval. I have therefore taken particular care to clear any information even verging on the confidential with the client, or, where this was impossible, to thoroughly disguise names and circumstances.

A number of my colleagues have made helpful criticisms and suggestions. Warren Cannon, D. Ronald Daniel, C. Lee Walton, and Arch Patton made particularly useful over-all contributions. Gilbert H. Clee, Raymond J. Klemmer, J. Roger Morrison, and Howard H. Williams contributed significantly to the chapters on planning. Roland Mann did a fine job of editing. To all of them I am indeed grateful.

Even though I adopted many of their suggestions, responsibility for the final result is, of course, mine. In fact, I am sure that—as management authorities in their own right—none of them wishes to be understood as agreeing with everything I say.

And now, because I believe this distillate of the success patterns of well-managed companies can be useful to any manager or prospective manager, I hope to sustain your "will to read" long enough to get through it!

Marvin Bower

CONTENTS

To Helen, who was so understanding of my absences in gathering the material and so inspiring in her encouragement that I try to make something useful from it.

1

"Where There's a Will . . ."

A few years ago I was asked to give a talk to a group of investment bankers and brokers about managing their type of business. In gathering material for the talk, I gained new insight into the importance of the *will to manage* as an ingredient for success in managing *any* business.

I interviewed about a dozen partners in leading investment banking and brokerage firms. Almost to a man, they told me that they and their partners could not give much attention to the work of managing their firms because they were too busy with "production"—attracting new customers, arranging for new issues, handling customer orders, and the like. In fact, several of these leaders declared with pride that they did not believe in "formal" management. Many of them seemed to equate management with paper shuffling by operating personnel in the back office.

Clearly, partners in these firms work hard and effectively, but chiefly as individual performers—not as managers. However, since most investment banking firms are essentially small businesses, many of them are highly successful even though none of the partners pays much attention to the task of managing. But despite the successes of their firms, thoughtful partners were concerned. Here, for example, are the comments of some I interviewed:

> "I'm afraid the character of our firm is changing without our even knowing it. We just grab any piece of business that comes along."

> "We're doing very well—too well, in fact. We're so interested in today's profits and today's decisions on new issues that we don't spend enough time deciding what kind of a business we want to conduct and how to go about getting that kind of business profitably."

> "I've tried to get some of my more senior partners to give up production and spend their time on management. But we're doing so well that I'm a voice crying in the wilderness."

Incidentally, reactions to my talk from members of the Investment Bankers Association who heard or later read it indicate that these anxieties were widely shared in the business.

In the brokerage business, however, as contrasted with investment banking, sheer size has forced many senior partners to give close and specific attention to management processes as such. Consequently, a number of senior partners in brokerage firms *have* developed the will to manage, and some have already developed very good systems of management. Failures and forced mergers among brokerage firms are also giving new impetus to recognition that managing is a separate type of activity, requiring specialized attention to developing managing processes. Failures and forced mergers during good times are a high price to pay for neglecting managing processes.

The will to manage is essential to full success in any kind of business. In his great book, *My Years with General Motors*,[1] the late Alfred P. Sloan, Jr., tells of the brilliant exploits of William C. Durant in putting GM together. But, he says, "Mr. Durant was a great man with a great weakness—he could create but not administer. . . . That he should have conceived a General Motors and been unable himself in the long run to bring it off . . . is a tragedy of American industrial history." What Mr. Sloan brought to GM was the *will to manage.*

What keeps many otherwise outstanding top-management executives from "bringing it off" as well as they should is the lack of the will to manage.

The Will and the Way

Necessity can generate the will to manage in the top executives of any business. In turn, the will to manage usually produces organized effort to develop effective management processes. For, as the proverb has it, "Where there's a will, there's a way."

Before taking up the *will* to manage, however, let's be sure we are agreed on the meaning of management itself. The comments I have quoted from my interviews with the investment bankers suggest a good working definition: Managing is the activity or task of determining the objectives of an organization and then guiding the people and other resources of the organization in the successful achievement of those objectives.

Any business can be permitted to drift with the tides of circumstance, subject to the external and internal forces at work. Alternatively, it can be *managed.* As the new chief executive of a highly successful international business expressed it to me, "We're determined to control our growth, not just get swept along with it." That is the will to manage.

But the will to *manage* is not synonymous with the will to *succeed.* The desire to see their enterprises succeed is almost universal among chief executives and senior managers. Let me illustrate the difference by the case of a very large but only moderately successful Midwestern company. The chief executive has a fierce desire for company success and pays a high personal price to achieve it. He works long hours to keep on top of what is going on, and he makes daring competitive moves and brilliant decisions on major programs and capital expenditures. He directs far-reaching and effective drives to expand volume and to cut costs. He shifts positions and people frequently.

Despite the chief executive's dominant personality, this is not simply a case of one-man management. The company is much too large for that. Sound management methods are used in many of its individual departments. The latest techniques in sales, manufacturing, and finance are constantly being adopted. The company was an early user of computers and operations research techniques. In fact, so-called "modern management methods" are being utilized quite generally and effectively. But the chief executive himself gives little or no attention to the processes of *managing*.

As a result, expanding volume and cutting costs are the only objectives known down the line. And there is no shared strategy for achieving even these obvious goals. Lower-level executives wait for signals from above. They recognize the large hidden costs in the chief executive's sudden switches of priority, but there is no tradition of speaking out on such matters. So, without any managing principles to guide them, people simply wait for instructions.

Privately, most of them are convinced that the business would be much more successful if its brilliant chief executive would give more attention to developing and using managing processes as such. But he is so busy making operating decisions that he has no time to improve the company's managing processes or to shape them into anything even approximating a system. Although the company's results are good, compared with its competitors its success is not spectacular. But it does well enough so that the chief executive has not yet been forced to develop the *will to manage.*

If he did develop the will to manage, his own capabilities would be multiplied. The productive energies of hundreds of executives would be more fully unleashed and better harnessed. Profits would be stepped up sharply. In short, his intense will to succeed would produce even better results.

No, the will to succeed is not the same as the will to manage. Both are needed. But I believe that the will to manage is an essential forerunner of outstanding, long-term success for companies of more than 300 employees. In fact, the success of *any* company will be increased if its top managers possess, in addition to the will to *succeed,* a strong determination to *manage.* For if they do, they will give real attention to building and using managing processes to translate that determination into effective managing action. They will take steps to control the business instead of letting it control them.

In short, I believe that success in managing a business is determined largely by how effectively, resolutely, and consistently top management makes simple concepts work. Most executives shrink from the effort to inaugurate "scientific management" because they know instinctively that management cannot be "scientific." But the able executive knows that "organized and systematized management" is a thoroughly realistic way to make a company more successful.

The Manager's Dual Role

It should be recognized immediately that developing managing processes and making operating decisions are two separate and distinct activities. Making operating decisions is a responsibility of every manager, high or low. But the higher his position, the more important becomes another responsibility—that of building and improving managing processes as such. A foreman or district sales manager, for example, might devote 90 percent or more of his time to operating decisions and the balance to improving the managing processes of his unit. At the other end of the scale, the chief executive of a billion-dollar business might well devote 30 percent of his time to operating decisions and 70 percent to building and improving the managing processes of the company.

I know another Midwestern company—a billion-dollar, multi-division business—whose chief executive spends most of his time considering decisions that come up from below (division budgets and new plant investments, for example) and reviewing the performance of divisions. Since he takes little time for work of his own choice, over-all managing processes, as such, receive little attention; for example, he has repeatedly put off the task of developing fundamental programs for dealing with two low-return divisions. The proportion of his time this chief executive spends on operating decisions is about right for a middle manager. He is neglecting an important part of his job.

Any general executive, but especially the chief executive, has a responsibility to establish, nurture, and improve managing processes. He is not doing his full job when he confines himself to making decisions passed up to him, selecting subordinates, reviewing and coordinating the work of subordinates, and providing leadership. That is his *operating* work. Of course, it is important work—so important, interesting, and demanding that it can easily encroach on, or even crowd out, the chief executive's other vital work of building managing processes. Until he recognizes his dual role and develops an adequate *will* to manage, the general executive will not devote the time, energy, and thought required to find the *way* to manage.

To drive home this important point, let me give another illustration. On a late winter afternoon, I sat in the office of the president and chief executive of the dominant company in its industry. The working day was over, and the president was in a reflective mood. "Do you realize," he said, "that I have worked up from the bottom of this business, and nowhere along the line has anyone told me anything about how to be president? In fact, no one has even told me anything along the way about being an executive, although I've had some instruction in how to do each job."

What the president meant, of course, was that no one had told him anything about the processes of managing. Clearly, he was on top of his operating work of making decisions and providing leadership, and his business was enjoying healthy growth in volume, share-of-market, and profits. But he knew that these good results could somehow be made even better. Intuitively, he felt that there must be more to his job than making decisions, however important, and providing leadership, however dynamic. He was beginning to sense his responsibility to *build* managing processes as well as use them. In short, he was developing the will to manage and so was reaching for better ways to manage.

To sum up: the task of managing is not just achieving economic results through sound and creative operating decisions. It also includes the development of managing processes by which all members of the organization can contribute to achieving the objectives of the enterprise and assuring its success. To help him keep this second vital responsibility constantly in mind, every executive should frequently recall Mr. Sloan's searching assessment of William Durant: "He could create but not administer."

Managing by System

So, where there's a *will* to manage, there's a *way* to manage.

I believe that the best way to translate the will to manage into effective management action is through the system approach: the top managers build their own tailor-made management system fitted to the nature and needs of the company—and enforce the system resolutely in the daily conduct of the business.

By a management system, I mean a set of interacting and interdependent managing processes which, as system components, combine in a conceptually unified program, or approach, for managing. The system provides a conceptual framework of coordinated principles or guidelines that welds together the component managing processes. Functioning as part of the system, each individual process has leverage, because its effectiveness is multiplied. The result is a hard-hitting total effort that is more powerful than the sum of the parts.

People can always act more effectively when there are principles to guide them. Knowing what to do, they don't have to wait for instructions. And when the principles are welded together by a clearly understood system, action becomes even more purposeful and productive.

The concept underlying the system approach to managing— that of the different processes working together—is best conveyed, I have found, by the term "programmed management." To achieve the full power of programmed management, everyone involved must be aware of the system and understand the interaction of the processes. Managers at all levels should know the component processes and how they work individually and as part of the system. They should understand that because each process is part of the system of programmed management, each not only gathers strength from the other components but imparts strength to them as well.

Adherence to such a system reduces the proportion of expedient, *ad hoc* decisions. Even when a business has an effective tailor-made management system, there must still be many *ad hoc* decisions. But the proportion of such decisions will be substantially lower, because the system provides a set of coordinated guidelines for decision and action. Moreover, the system enables each individual decision and action to pack more purposeful power because it supports, and is supported by, other decisions and actions taken under the system.

Thus the will and the system operate in tandem to maximize success. The will generates the determination to build the system. Once established, the system translates the will into effective action. And effective action, in turn, strengthens the will to manage. As the brilliant chief executive of a large and rapidly growing business remarked, "We decided to get on top of our business by building a system to manage it—something we've never been able to do in any other way."

Other Approaches to Managing

The concept of programmed management comes alive more vividly when it is contrasted with other approaches to managing.

Ad hoc management: This approach is characterized by total lack of character, concept, or design. There are no principles to follow. Each decision is made independently, with little regard to objectives, strategy, policies, or other decisions. Traditional managing processes are used, of course, but there is no conscious effort to adhere to them and no effort at all to develop and integrate them. Instead, those who should manage the business are carried along by it. Expediency prevails, and the only over-all policy is drift. There is no will to manage; there is only a desire to make a profit.

No company, of course, employs a purely *ad hoc* approach to managing. To some extent, actions will be guided by "experience" and precedent. Some kind of guiding philosophy—even if it is only "doing what the boss wants"—will evolve to provide a sense of order for the people working together. In the company where the programmed management approach provides a co-ordinated set of principles to guide decision making and action, there is simply less need for expediency.

Day-to-day management: There is less expediency in this approach than in *ad hoc* management, but managers are still too interested in short-term profits to consider the long-range implications of day-to-day decisions. Hence, they fail to gear current action to any long-range strategy. Day-to-day managing often produces profits, but seldom long-term success.

Piecemeal management: This approach reflects some will to manage, but there is no attempt to integrate managing processes. At one time, top managers put on a drive for volume. At another, they put on the pressure for expense reduction. These switches in emphasis confuse managers and supervisors and reduce the likelihood of achieving maximum success.

Personal management: Where this approach prevails, top management puts primary emphasis on the personal abilities, attitudes, and desires of individuals. Instead of expecting people to adapt their actions and attitudes to the coordinated set of principles that constitute the management system, management methods are adapted to individuals. Policy may be altered or responsibility increased or diminished to suit a man's abilities or his attitudes. Keeping people "happy" and holding down turnover are major management concerns.

This approach is beguiling because of its sweet reasonableness: It is favored by executives who don't believe in "formal" management because "we want to have a happy family around here." The alternative to personal management, they may suggest, is to straitjacket the organization with inflexible requirements that make no allowance for the human factor.

In point of fact, this is merely a convenient rationalization. Systematized management does, of course, permit reasonable accommodation of differences in individual abilities. And personal management, instead of making people really happy and productive, simply creates confusion. Lacking principle and fairness, it also lacks appeal to able people, who don't want personal accommodation that is not in the company's interests.

Personal power management: This is an invidious form of personal management. The decisive factor in this approach is the relative standing or power of individuals, based on seniority, tenure, popularity, or influence with top management ("management by crony"). Top managers adjust their decisions to fit the power structure and appease the people who count. Thus, top management of an advertising agency may alter policy to suit an account executive who has a key account "in his pocket."

This approach promotes internal politics, since people soon come to recognize that the way to get ahead is to develop some personal power position that can be used as a lever. Personal power management, of course, lacks principle and objectivity, and high-caliber people will put up with only a minimum amount of it.

One-man management: This well-known approach can override any other, including systematized management. Its hallmark is an overly dominant chief executive who makes most of the important decisions and hence is a poor delegator. Instead of taking timely action in accordance with policy, people down the line wait for orders. Feedback is limited, and the man at the top becomes isolated from facts and attitudes. People fail to develop, and continuity of effective management is seldom provided for. Fortunately, the unsoundness of this approach is usually so obvious, even to the "one man" himself, that the chances for correction are greater than in most of the other approaches I have discussed.

All these alternatives to programmed management have two

major deficiences in common. First, the various managing processes are not clearly defined and therefore cannot be developed and learned by the people down the line. Hence, guidelines for decisions and action are lacking, and coordinated action cannot be fairly enforced.

Second and more important, the interactions among the managing processes are not recognized and articulated. For example, too little attention is given to determining whether, and precisely how, a proposed policy or organizational change will help achieve company or division objectives. Once a sound policy or organizational change has been decided on, too little effort is made to show people the reasoning behind it. The interactions between the managing processes are not talked about enough, if indeed they are recognized at all.

In short, these other management approaches are amorphous or mushy. They lack principle. They are indefinite and unclear. They are unfair to able people—people who want to know where they stand, who want to be productive, who don't seek unauthorized power, and who don't want accommodation. Compared to programmed management, these other approaches are ineffectual guidance mechanisms and poor enforcement mediums. They neither stimulate the will to manage nor translate the will to manage into effective action.

Overcoming Inhibitors of Management Will

In contrast, programmed management has built-in values that help make the will to manage effective at all levels by overcoming deterrents to its development and use.

Long observation has convinced me that the primary deterrent to developing a stronger will to manage is the natural reluctance of most managers to discipline their subordinates or to injure their feelings. Yet the whole history of group activity in any civilization shows that productivity of the individual member of any group can only be assured through dedication and/or discipline. To put it another way: Getting the individual to give his best efforts toward achieving group objectives must be *inspired* and/or *required.*

An executive is naturally reluctant to *require* performance when it seems somehow unfair or awkward to make a particular demand or enforce it through some form of discipline. In such circumstances the temptation is strong to let the awkward matter pass and to act expediently, or accept some compromise with principle that will be less likely to upset the individual concerned. Unfortunately, delay or compromise seldom solves the problem, and the longer the discipline is postponed the more rigorous it may have to be. Moreover, the costs of delay and the resentments from sterner discipline are likely to inhibit the will to manage even more.

My thesis, therefore, is that any top management can fashion traditional managing processes into an individualized system of programmed management—a system which, properly adhered to, will stimulate *inspiring* and facilitate *requiring* by making it easier for managers to make decisions and require actions of their subordinates.

Let me make that point another way, because it is important: Any company or division can develop a system of management, tailored to its own needs, that will (1) *inspire* greater dedication to company objectives, goals, and programs among people at all levels; and (2) make it easier, fairer, and less awkward for managers to impose the discipline necessary to *require* company personnel to adhere to company philosophy and to follow the strategic plans, policies, and procedures in accordance with established standards. Such a system provides backbone for the will to manage and makes it more effective. And the will to manage, in turn, strengthens the system.

The great British prime minister, Benjamin Disraeli, once said, "The secret of success is constancy to purpose." By inspiring and requiring people to adhere to a coordinated set of principles that are geared to company objectives, programmed management helps to build and strengthen "constancy to purpose."

Although the system makes "requiring" easier, it also tends to make it less necessary. Capable managers, therefore, will use the system primarily to *inspire* people to work effectively. The better the system, the more freedom it makes possible for the individual, because—knowing what to do and how and when to do it—he will not often need to be told, ordered, or otherwise "required."

Thus, while systematized management may sound restrictive, in practice quite the reverse is true. The system frees people to work on their own. It allows them a greater degree of self-direction and self-control. In other words, it promotes self-government. The best source of energy for a management system, in fact, is the self-governing initiative of the people whose activities it guides. That is why able people *like* working under a system of programmed management—and why they work with greater effectiveness and zest.

A soundly constructed management system focuses management's primary attention on accomplishment of purpose rather than perfection of method, on performance rather than procedure, and on results rather than rules. Such a focus keeps the business more responsive to its environment and to the future.

I hope, therefore, that the word "system" as applied to management will not suggest restrictive rules and bureaucratic control. A sound management system, in fact, frees people from the smothering effects of bureaucracy, because it stimulates dynamism.

A soundly constructed management system is enduring—yet it facilitates change. It provides a flexible structure or framework within which the various components can be changed without upsetting the balance of the system itself. Thus new policies, plans, and programs can be more readily introduced, understood, assimilated, and acted on. The system just keeps rolling along even when the components are being quite substantially changed, and recognition of this fact creates an internal environment that is more receptive to change. In a system-managed business, therefore, people are more ready to take change in stride and to make it effective sooner. In a period when technological change is accelerating, greater internal flexibility and responsiveness are valuable management resources.

Finally, a sound management system is simple in structure and use. The components are traditional management processes. The key to the system is an understanding of how each of the processes functions and how each interrelates with the others. Thus a company managed by system develops a rhythm which increases the value of its management both as a competitive tool and as a capital asset.

Managing Processes: System Components

To be sure we have a common understanding of the components from which a management system is built, let's take a brief look at the classical managing processes—the ways things get done effectively through group action. In my experience, few managers outside the largest and most successful companies have a real working understanding of these processes and their meanings. Only sophisticated managers recognize that all purposeful management action involves one or more of these basic processes.

These processes are common denominators in managing any group. Even an undertaking as simple as a family picnic is a group effort calling for many management decisions: when and where to go, what equipment to take, whether there should be an exception to the regular bedtimes for the children, what each child should do to help get ready, and what standards of behavior the children are expected to maintain. In fact, before the picnic is over, nearly every traditional managing process will have been called into play. Essentially the same processes must be used in achieving the purposes of any group or organization—family, church, school, government, or business.

By the same token, the managing processes of any enterprise, from an international oil company to the local hardware store, should be fashioned with particular concern for the primary common denominator: people. No business, regardless of type or size, can maximize its success in the long run unless its managing processes deal effectively with the ambitions, abilities, strengths, indifferences, inertias, weaknesses, fears, and foibles of people.

Of the four "M's" that have become classic in the literature of management—men, materials, money, and management—the core element is men, for it is men who plan, decide, and act. The function of management (specifically, of the management system) is to get people to do these things effectively in the interests of the enterprise—hopefully, because they like and want to. The system must help them determine what activities to perform and how to perform those activities well. Finally, the system should help the company attract and hold high-caliber people. The focus of this book, then, is people—and people are central to most of the managing processes I discuss.

Fourteen basic and well-known managing processes make up

the components from which a management system for any business can be fashioned.

1. *Setting objectives:* Deciding on the business or businesses in which the company or division should engage and on other fundamentals that shall guide and characterize the business, such as continuous growth. An objective is typically enduring and timeless.

2. *Planning strategy:* Developing concepts, ideas, and plans for achieving objectives successfully, and for meeting and beating competition. Strategic planning is part of the total planning process that includes management and operational planning.

3. *Establishing goals:* Deciding on achievement targets shorter in time range or narrower in scope than the objectives, but designed as specific sub-objectives in making operational plans for carrying out strategy.

4. *Developing a company philosophy:* Establishing the beliefs, values, attitudes, and unwritten guidelines that add up to "the way we do things around here."

5. *Establishing policies:* Deciding on plans of action to guide the performance of all major activities in carrying out strategy in accordance with company philosophy.

6. *Planning the organization structure:* Developing the plan of organization—the "harness" that helps people pull together in performing activities in accordance with strategy, philosophy, and policies.

7. *Providing personnel:* Recruiting, selecting, and developing people—including an adequate proportion of high-caliber talent—to fill the positions provided for in the organization plan.

8. *Establishing procedures:* Determining and prescribing how all important and recurrent activities shall be carried out.

9. *Providing facilities:* Providing the plant, equipment, and other physical facilities required to carry on the business.

10. *Providing capital:* Making sure the business has the money and credit needed for physical facilities and working capital.

11. *Setting standards:* Establishing measures of performance that will best enable the business to achieve its long-term objectives successfully.

12. *Establishing management programs and operational plans:* Developing programs and plans governing activities and the use of resources which—when carried out in accordance with established strategy, policies, procedures, and standards—will enable people to achieve particular goals. These are phases of the total planning process that includes strategic planning.

13. *Providing control information:* Supplying facts and figures to help people follow the strategy, policies, procedures, and programs; to keep alert to forces at work inside and outside the business; and to measure their own performance against established plans and standards.

14. *Activating people:* Commanding and motivating people up and down the line to act in accordance with philosophy, policies, procedures, and standards in carrying out the plans of the company.

Fashioning these fourteen components into a tailor-made management system is the building job of every chief executive and every general executive. To support, follow, and enforce the system is a vital part of every top manager's operating job—and of managers and supervisors at every level.

The value of careful attention to fundamentals has been demonstrated in many types of activity where success requires that people work effectively together in groups. Take, for example, the 1964 National Football League championship game. The Baltimore Colts went into the game heavy favorites over the Cleveland Browns—but the Browns won 27–0. Asked later how they had done it, Coach Blanton Collier told reporters: "We went right back to fundamentals." The first two weeks before the game, he explained, had been spent reteaching basic football to professionals who had just completed a winning 14-game season. In business the "champions" also give careful attention to fundamentals.

Obviously, fundamentals pay off only if they are actually used on the job. The Cleveland Browns would not have won the championship game if the fundamentals they had practiced for two weeks to perfect had not been superbly executed during the game. The importance of a real application of fundamentals in managing a corporation successfully has been stated well by Frederic G. Donner, chairman of General Motors. Here is what Mr. Donner said in a lecture made shortly after he reported that GM profits in 1965 were in excess of $2 billion on sales of $20.7 billion:

> Principles, policies, and procedures are effective only insofar as the management of an enterprise understands them and relates them in a meaningful way to the day-to-day operations of the business. Application is the key and accomplishment is the final test. In the case of General Motors, I believe the results have justified this method of operation.[2]

I hope to show that the system approach to managing helps any management substantially in achieving the kind of application of fundamentals that Mr. Donner describes and says is the key.

Measuring Success

Since the principal reason for employing the system approach is to help the top managers operate a company more successfully, it is important to agree on the meaning of "success." I believe that business success can best be measured by three standards:

1. *Growth in volume and share-of-market:* Are the dollar sales of the business growing year by year? Is it constantly increasing its share of the volume of business done in the products and/or services it offers for sale? These are measures of competitive position.

2. *Long-term return on invested capital:* Among the various measures of profitability, this seems to best reflect the interests of shareholders, employees, and the national economy.

3. *Continuity of effective management:* No company can be fully successful unless it develops managers capable of continuing the business successfully "in perpetuity."

There are other measures of business success: product franchise, employee attitudes, public standing, and social responsibility. But my observations of successful businesses convince me that any company with a growing volume and share-of-market, increasing long-term return on investment, and continuity of effective management will be required to meet those other tests of success as well.

To be successful a company must also be flexible. Top management must keep the business adjusted to its environment, employ the latest manufacturing processes, keep costs down, take advantage of the latest management techniques, and so on. Programmed management is designed to help top managers detect the need for change and make the necessary adjustments to new conditions. It facilitates the adoption of improvements in management techniques. New methods can easily be slotted into the system. And, through its integrated character, the system itself assures that the new techniques will be employed in a balanced manner, without the over-emphasis that frequently is given to something new.

The dramatic profit turn-around of Eastern Air Lines between 1963 and 1965 is fine testimony to the power and flexibility of systematized management in the hands of strong leadership. In 1963, after four years of steady decline, Eastern Air Lines reported a deficit of $37.8 million. Two years later, it was not only out of the red but into the black to the tune of $29.7 million in profits after taxes. This outstanding result was attained in an industry with an exceedingly rapid rate of technological change, requiring the use of the most advanced management techniques.

Under the leadership of a new president, Floyd Hall, Eastern's new, capable, and aggressive management team regained success by putting well-known management principles to work in a systematized, dynamic, and well-articulated manner. Clearly it was Mr. Hall's will to manage that gave backbone, purpose, and drive to the new program. But, as he has said publicly, the result was attained through nothing more magical than applying traditional management methods. He even had a motion picture produced to show the importance and value of doing simple things consistently and well.

Programmed management, then, is an approach well suited to achieving success under changing conditions. There is nothing rigid or inflexible about it. Like any other approach to management, it is no better than the people who use it. But management by system encourages people of all levels of ability to put out their best efforts with initiative, resourcefulness, and zest.

The nature and benefits of programmed management will become clearer as we consider its principal components. But let's begin with company philosophy since it has a built-in influence on everything else.

2

Company Philosophy:
"The Way We Do Things around Here"

I have an abstract painting in my office that I bought in London off the Piccadilly fence. In that open-air mart, which operates on weekends, the artists sell their own works. Judged by the $43 price, my painting is not great art. But it has delightful swirls, angles, and other abstract forms, all in bright colors. And when Mr. Eves, the artist, told me the title—"Forces at Work"—I bought it immediately.

With a little metal plate bearing the title and the artist's name, the painting is a constant reminder to me that any successful organization must give continuing attention to keeping adjusted to the forces affecting it—that is, to the forces-at-work element of its philosophy. But before discussing that element, let us examine the whole concept of company philosophy as a system component and identify other important elements of a successful philosophy.

Meaning and Elements of Company Philosophy

Over the years, I have noticed that some executives—particularly top-management executives in the most successful com-

panies—frequently refer to "our philosophy." They may speak
of something that "our philosophy calls for," or of some action
taken in the business that is "not in accordance with our philosophy." In mentioning "our philosophy," they assume that everyone knows what "our philosophy" is.

As the term is most commonly used, it seems to stand for the
basic beliefs that people in the business are expected to hold and
be guided by—informal, unwritten guidelines on how people
should perform and conduct themselves. Once such a philosophy
crystallizes, it becomes a powerful force indeed. When one person tells another, "That's not the way we do things around here,"
the advice had better be heeded. And when a superior says that
to a subordinate, it had better be taken as an order.

In dealing with the concept as I find it used in practice by
leading executives, the literature on company philosophy is
neither very extensive nor very satisfactory. But one dictionary
definition of philosophy does apply: "general laws that furnish
the rational explanation of anything." In this sense, a company
philosophy evolves as a set of laws or guidelines that gradually
become established, through trial and error or through leadership, as expected patterns of behavior.

In discussing the philosophy of International Business
Machines Corporation, Thomas J. Watson, Jr., the chairman,
says:

> I firmly believe that any organization, in order to survive
> and achieve success, must have a sound set of beliefs on which
> it premises all its policies and actions.
>
> Next, I believe that the most important single factor in
> corporate success is faithful adherence to those beliefs. . . .
>
> In other words, the basic philosophy, spirit and drive of an
> organization have far more to do with its relative achievements
> than do technological or economic resources, organizational
> structure, innovation and timing. All these things weigh heavily

on success. But they are, I think, transcended by how strongly the people in the organization believe in its basic precepts and how faithfully they carry them out.[1]

Some typical examples of basic beliefs that serve as guidelines to action will clarify the concept. Although such basic beliefs inevitably vary from company to company, here are five that I find recurring frequently in the most successful corporations:

1. Maintenance of high ethical standards in external and internal relationships is essential to maximum success.

2. Decisions should be based on facts, objectively considered —what I call the fact-founded, thought-through approach to decision making.

3. The business should be kept in adjustment with the forces at work in its environment.

4. People should be judged on the basis of their performance, not on nationality, personality, education, or personal traits and skills.

5. The business should be administered with a sense of competitive urgency.

These five common-denominator elements—combined with other beliefs—are informal supplements to the more formal processes of management. A brief discussion of each will show how useful and how powerful a company philosophy can be, once it provides effective guidelines for "the way we do things around here."

High Ethical Standards

In dealing with the value of high ethical standards in a business, I don't want to belabor the obvious. But I do want to point up a few nuances that sometimes escape even executives of high principle.

Since the whole purpose of a system of management is to

inspire and require people to carry out company strategy by following policies, procedures, and programs, no management should overlook the set of built-in guidelines that every employee with a good family background brings to the job. Since anyone who has been well trained in Judaic-Christian ethics instinctively acts in accordance with those principles, it is sheer shortsightedness for any management to overlook the great practical value of these powerful guidelines of conduct.

The business with high ethical standards has three primary advantages over competitors whose standards are lower:

■ A business of high principle generates greater drive and effectiveness because people know that they can do the *right* thing decisively and with confidence. When there is any doubt about what action to take, they can rely on the guidance of ethical principles. I can think of three companies—the leaders in their respective industries—whose inner administrative drive emanates largely from the fact that everyone feels confident that he can safely do the right thing immediately. And he also knows that any action which is even slightly unprincipled will be generally condemned.

■ A business of high principle attracts high-caliber people more easily, thereby gaining a basic competitive and profit edge. A high-caliber person, because he prefers to associate with people he can trust, favors the business of principle; and he avoids the employer whose practices are questionable. So, in taking his first job or in changing jobs, he takes the trouble to find out. For this reason, companies that do not adhere to high ethical standards must actually maintain a higher level of compensation to attract and hold people of ability. A few large companies have to "reach" for able people with higher compensation simply because low standards of relationships among people produce a "jungle" atmosphere in which it is less agreeable to work.

■ A business of high principle develops better and more profitable relations with customers, competitors, and the general public, because it can be counted on to do the right thing at all times. By the consistently ethical character of its actions, it builds a favorable image. In choosing among suppliers, customers resolve their doubts in favor of such a company. Competitors are less likely to comment unfavorably on it. And the general public is more likely to be open-minded toward its actions and receptive to its advertising and other communications.

Consider the example of Avon Products, Inc., the house-to-house cosmetics business. Since 1954 Avon's net profit has been increasing at an average of over 19 percent a year, compounded, and in 1963 its return on investment reached 34 percent. According to an article in the December 1964 issue of *Fortune,* Avon's founder, David H. McConnell, "was resolved to be different from the swarms of itinerant peddlers who were at that time selling goods of indifferent quality to housewives, and then moving on, rarely to be seen again." The founder's son carried on his father's belief in high principle. Citing comments by competitors and suppliers on the company's high ethical standards, the article notes that Avon's present chairman, John A. Ewald, its president, Wayne Hicklin, and a top-management executive now deceased "did a great deal to ensure that the McConnells' high ethical standards would continue to be diffused throughout the organization as it expanded."

There should be no need to dwell on these well-recognized values. But too often, I find, they tend to be taken for granted. My point in mentioning them is to urge executives to actively seek ways of making high principle a more explicit element in their company philosophy. No one likes to declaim about his honesty and trustworthiness; but the leaders of a company can profitably articulate, within the organization, their determination that everyone shall adhere to high standards of ethics. That is the best foundation for a profit-making company philosophy and a profitable system of management.

Fact-founded Decision Making

Some readers will recall the television mystery series, "Dragnet," which once had a high rating. The hero who always solved the mystery was Friday, a detective of the Los Angeles police force. In working on each case, Friday and his partner called at the homes or apartments of a number of witnesses. Often, if a woman answered the door, she would be frightened when they showed her their credentials. Friday would always reassure her: "Ma'am, we're just trying to get the facts."

Every decision maker should "try to get the facts." Obvious though it may seem, the key importance of a fact-founded approach to decision making as an element in company philosophy cannot be overstressed.

To some degree, of course, every company does use a fact-founded approach to decision making. It must, or it would promptly fail. Like so many other management concepts, however, the value of the fact-founded approach depends on the degree and effectiveness of its use. As one gauge of this, how often do you hear people talking about "who's right" instead of "what's right"?

My observations in numerous businesses over the years convince me that only the most successful companies really use facts adequately and with full effectiveness in developing strategic plans and making decisions. Too many executives get fixed attitudes on common issues, typifying the cliché, "My mind is made up—don't bother me with the facts." Too many executives —even some successful ones—come to value their own opinions and judgments so highly that they ignore or underestimate facts.

Some even resent it if their subordinates call their attention to facts that suggest action contrary to their own fixed ideas.

In one company—the volume leader in its industry—suppression of the facts as guides to action resulted in a gradual loss of profit position. Because of top management's fixed attitudes about the company's time-honored distribution system, dedication to that system became the cornerstone of company philosophy. Concentrating on volume and ignoring facts about product performance and user attitudes, management let each distributor have his own way as long as he maintained share-of-market in his territory.

Finally, a few years ago, profits declined so sharply that a new chief executive took over. He diagnosed the basic problem as "a wrong attitude of mind" among company executives. His primary solution was to insist that all plans and decisions be based on open-minded consideration of the facts. This brought about major changes in products and distribution and some decline in volume, but it also produced a substantial improvement in profits. Over the long term, that company's share-of-market is bound to increase, because its products now perform better and customer service has been improved. Nearly all these changes have come about simply because executives at all levels are now in the habit of "getting the facts," evaluating them objectively, and acting accordingly.

The example of General Motors, the world's largest private enterprise and, by any standards, a most successful one, drives the point home. *U.S. News and World Report,* in its issue of December 30, 1949, carried a copyrighted interview with Charles E. Wilson, then president of GM and later U.S. Secretary of Defense. In the interview, which was held because of "the widespread interest in the management of large-scale enterprises,"

Mr. Wilson, made these comments on the importance of the factual approach to decision making:

> Since reasonable men in the presence of the facts don't have too much trouble to reach an agreement or to arrive at the right decision for an activity, we start out by trying to get the facts about any problem that we have at hand. We try not to make up our minds too quickly about what we are going to do. So we do develop the facts, and everybody who can reasonably contribute has a chance to do so. We don't delay too long. If a house is on fire, I'll turn the hose on right away—but, otherwise, we take a little time.

Six years later, in 1955, a Senate subcommittee investigating the dealer practices of the automobile industry asked Harlow Curtice, then president of GM, to testify. In the course of his statement to the subcommittee, Mr. Curtice gave four reasons for the success of GM. One of them was the fact-founded approach, and here is what he said about it:

> Now we come to the second fundamental reason for the success of General Motors—our approach to problems. It is really an attitude of mind. It might be defined as bringing the research point of view to bear on all phases of the business. This involves, first, assembling all the facts, second, analysis of where the facts appear to point, and third, *courage to follow the trail indicated even if it leads into unfamiliar and unexplored territory.* This point of view is never satisfied with things as they are. It assumes that everything and anything—whether it be product, process, method, procedure, or social or human relations—can be improved. [Italics supplied.]
>
> I have tried to think of a single term to describe this attitude, and I think perhaps the closest is the *inquiring* mind.
>
> It may appear to be boastful, but I truly believe that in General Motors we have developed to a unique degree this

attitude of the inquiring mind. We are always seeking ways to make things better and do things better.

In 1964, 9 years after the Curtice testimony, Mr. Sloan's book about General Motors made it clear that in developing the philosophy of that great company he stressed the factual approach to decision making. Here is what Mr. Sloan says:

> An essential aspect of our management philosophy is the factual approach to business judgment. The final act of business judgment is of course intuitive. Perhaps there are formal ways of improving the logic of business strategy, or policy making. But the big work behind business judgment is in finding and acknowledging the facts and circumstances concerning technology, the market, and the like in their continuously changing forms. . . .
>
> In the corporation there is an atmosphere of objectivity and enjoyment of enterprise. *One of the corporation's great strengths is that it was designed to be an objective organization, as distinguished from the type that gets lost in the subjectivity of personalities.* . . . [Italics supplied.]
>
> It is imperative for the health of the organization that it always tends to rise above subjectivity.[2]

Each of these three public statements, made by three chief executives of GM over a period of 15 years, stresses the fact-founded approach as a major reason for the company's success. And I can testify that in day-to-day decision making, the attention to facts in that company is just as real and just as effective as these three chief executives suggest.

A factual approach to decision making can and should be talked about, but it cannot be legislated. Action in getting, analyzing, and following the facts is the only way to establish the fact-founded approach.

Ideally, the job of building in the fact-founded approach

starts at the top. The higher the executive, the more powerful will his example be. But the head of any department or even of any section can build the factual approach into his unit. If he insists on facts and acts on facts, his subordinates will do likewise. Both their morale and their performance will improve.

In building and using the fact-founded approach, every executive should realize how easy it is to shut off the flow of facts. He need only indicate that his mind is closed, that his experience cannot be disputed, or that he prefers to make judgments without facts. Then, depending on how forcefully he has rejected the fact-founded approach, the flow of facts from his subordinates will be reduced or even shut off. Of course, they will not tell him that they are withholding facts. Instead, they will simply echo his judgments, cloaking their agreement in a factual aura that deludes the boss into thinking he is making fact-founded decisions.

In large-scale organizations, the factual approach must be constantly nurtured by high-level executives. The more layers of authority through which facts must pass before they reach the decision maker, the greater the danger that they will be suppressed, modified, or softened so as not to displease the "brass." For this reason, high-level executives must keep *reaching* for facts or soon they won't know what is going on. Unless they make visible efforts to seek and act on facts, major problems will not be brought to their attention, the quality of their decisions will decline, and the business will gradually get out of touch with its environment.

I know one large company where the chief executive is so dominant and his belief in his own judgment so pronounced, that people all the way down the line are busy guessing what he would do and what he is likely to decide. Since unwelcome facts often do not reach him, he makes costly mistakes. The quality of his decisions could easily be better if he kept the fact channels open so that facts might flow up to him.

But no upward flow is an easy flow. In a large company especially, the chief executive can easily isolate himself from harsh external and internal facts and make decisions in a pleasant vacuum, while the company heads straight for trouble. In lesser degrees, the same possibility of isolation from reality exists at lower levels of the executive ladder.

Thus, building and maintaining the fact-founded approach calls for constant nurturing and rebuilding. If it is to be a fully effective force in successful management, the fact-founded approach must be *used*. Abuse and under-use lead quickly to atrophy.

When it is fully developed and actively applied at all levels, however, the fact-founded approach is a management instrument of great power. Here are some of the values it produces:

■ *Better decisions.* When facts are overlooked, ignored, or under-valued, they have a way of inexorably reasserting themselves. No matter how good his judgment, a decision maker can make a good decision only if, like Detective Friday, he "gets the facts." By keeping minds open and alert, a factual atmosphere stimulates better thinking, and thus causes a cumulative buildup in better decision making.

■ *Greater flexibility.* When the fact-founded approach has been established, plans and decisions change with new facts. This provides automatic justification for the executive who must change his prior decision; in truth, he is acting *consistently* because, in both decisions, he is simply being guided by the facts. In such an atmosphere, readjustment to reality is continuous; and that is certainly an essential ingredient of successful management.

With the increasing tempo of technological change, the fact-founded approach becomes an even more essential ingredient of successful management. Adjustment to change is simply an adjustment to new conditions, i.e., new facts. As Mr. Curtice said, a company must have the "courage to follow the trail indicated even if it leads into unfamiliar and unexplored territory."

■ *Higher morale.* Inevitably, company-wide respect for facts and their objective evaluation lowers the barriers between levels of authority. When everyone feels that "we're in this together, to find and face the facts, and to do whatever the facts dictate," the upward flow of facts is stimulated, and subordinates are encouraged to speak up. *Esprit de corps* is quickly evident in a company where the fact-founded approach is fully practiced. When everyone is trying to determine "what's right," not "who's right," discussion replaces argument and personal differences and personality conflicts are minimized.

Forces at Work

One element of a successful company philosophy is a sensitivity to the external forces affecting the business and to the need for adjustment to the environment in which the company operates. This is really part of the fact-founded approach, because the forces affecting a business *are* facts—and important ones.

The most successful executives make continuous efforts to keep the operations of their companies adjusted to the external forces affecting the objectives, strategy, products, people, and plants of the business. The external forces at work may be economic, competitive, technological, social, or political. When laws, market conditions, customer values, competitive thrust, or public attitudes change, the business must change its strategic plans, products, policies, facilities, structure, and/or people. When costs rise, changes must be made in prices, production methods, plants, wage rates, overhead expense, or organization. And if the external changes are substantial, the adjustment must be strategic, not tactical.

The classic case of the dinosaur was well stated in a speech by Thomas C. Dillon, president of Batten, Barton, Durstine & Osborn, Inc.:

> Like all living things, a business must adapt itself to its environment, and when it fails to adapt itself to changes in that environment, it dies.
>
> The business that died out was much like the dinosaur. . . . When faced with major changes in earth's climate and competitive behavior of other animal and plant life, the dinosaur was unable to make strategic adaptation to its environment. . . . For centuries businesses have lived and died much like the dinosaur, unable to adapt themselves strategically to their environment with the speed necessary to maintain survival.[3]

Successful management is outward-looking management. It seeks facts that indicate the need for change; it is sensitive to its environment, and especially to the customer needs, values, and attitudes on which the success of the business ultimately rests. It faces problems. It seizes new opportunities.

Classic extremes of the need for adjustment are found in the ice company and the carriage manufacturer. As the electric refrigerator replaced the icebox, some ice companies managed to shift to selling coal and later oil, but most went out of business. And only a few carriage manufacturers were able to survive the onslaught of the automobile.

A 1964 study by the First National City Bank of New York underscores the necessity of strategic adjustment for continuing success. Analyzing the lists of the 100 largest U.S. manufacturing corporations (in terms of total assets) from 1919 to 1963, the study shows that fewer than half the companies remained in the top 100 during this period. Even between 1948 and 1963, one out of every five companies slipped from the top 100 category, and the rankings of most of the others changed radically.

In reporting on the study, the bank's *Monthly Economic Letter* for August 1964 observed: "The surviving companies are largely those that have proven themselves adaptable to changes in the economy. . . . Thus, a top position in the economy is neither automatic nor permanent but requires continuous attention to the changing needs of the nation."

One of the great things about our competitive profit-and-loss system, of course, is the way its thrust fosters change, benefiting people through the new and/or improved product, process or service, and/or lower prices. But success requires that a company not only furnish its own thrust but keep alert to outside forces, capitalize on new opportunities, and make the necessary strategic and tactical adjustments in its products, services, facilities, operations, finances, people, and prices. The most successful businesses are sensitive to external forces at work and make such adjustments quickly. An alert and flexible business models itself on the chameleon, not the dinosaur.

You may not be the possessor of a painting that constantly reminds you to keep looking outward for external forces affecting your business. But to ensure maximum success you must somehow keep the eyes and ears of the company alerted to external changes that either offer opportunties or constitute threats. Of course, keeping the business adjusted to such changes is one purpose of a system of management.

Judging People on Performance

Successful companies judge their people on the basis of their actions and achievements, not their personal qualities and skills. Performance evaluation is a powerful element in a company *how?*

philosophy, because it is more factual and less subjective than quality-and-skill evaluation. Thus, this element is closely related to the fact-founded approach.

Even hiring decisions are soundest when they are based as much as possible on the individual's past performance. Of course, when filling a specific position it is wise to specify the personal qualities and skills that the person needs to perform the work of the position well. But whether a given person actually possesses those qualities and skills is best decided on the basis of what he has actually *done,* as reflected in his record of achievement at school or in his previous positions.

The great psychologist, John Dewey, is reported to have believed that a person's character and basic abilities are largely determined by the time he is 3 years old. Although this is a discouraging thought to parents, it has relevance in business. Certainly company experience with which I am familiar supports the proposition that "we are becoming today what we will be tomorrow."

I believe, therefore, that what a person has done in the past is the most reliable indicator of what he is likely to do in the future. If he was an effective thinker, performer, or leader as a child, in college, or in his previous jobs, he is likely to bring the same qualities to the position for which he is being evaluated. (A person's success pattern is usually a more reliable basis for prediction than the success pattern of a business, because even an effective management may fail to provide the business with an equally effective successor management.)

And once a person has been employed, what he does is clearly the most reliable guide for approval or disapproval and for decisions on compensation and advancement. A "good" personality, or a "good" education, for example, means little if it is not reflected in superior on-the-job performance. Performance is also the soundest basis for a separation decision.

Another important reason for building this element into a company philosophy is its widely accepted fairness. Judging a person on the basis of his performance squares with Judaic-Christian ethics and appeals to Anglo-Saxon sporting instincts. Thus, the person with the fine appearance and personality is given no intentional advantage.

Because of its recognized fairness, the practice of judging people by their performance increases the likelihood that superiors will apply to their subordinates the discipline necessary to require them to follow the management system. Thus, judging people by their performance helps overcome the natural reluctance of people to apply direct discipline.

In subsequent chapters I discuss other system components that facilitate effective discipline. But none is more important than establishing as one element of a company's philosophy the principle that people shall be judged by what they do and how well they do it. This approach to evaluating people should become an integral part of "the way we do things around here."

Sense of Competitive Urgency

Based on my own comparisons of the administration of leading American and British companies, I believe that the greater management effectiveness achieved by leading American companies is due chiefly to the greater sense of competitive urgency that pervades our most successful businesses. Addressing the Industrial Copartnership Association in London, in 1961, H.R.H. The Duke of Edinburgh put it this way: "Foreign competition is real; it is going to get tougher, so that if we want to be prosperous we have simply got to get down to it and work for it. The rest of the world most certainly does not owe us a living."

Certainly management technique is less important than competitive urgency. Even the most advanced management methods will not be fully effective unless these techniques are adopted and administered with a sense of competitive urgency. Talking to an international management congress, the late Charles E. Wilson, then president of GM, put it this way:

> Too frequently visitors to America are overly impressed by our assembly lines and our progressive mass-production manufacturing methods and are inclined to think that the physical organization of the work is the essence of our American production system. They will be confusing the form with the substance if they believe that simply by installing assembly lines and progressive manufacturing they will automatically get the same efficient production and low cost that American industry achieves. If they do not understand and apply the other fundamentals of our system at the same time, they will be greatly disappointed with the results they get. . . .
>
> The first essential of our American industrial system is the acceptance by Americans of competition. The responsibility for individual competition as well as competition between companies and business organizations stimulates the millions of Americans to contribute to better ways of doing things and to accomplish more with the same amount of human effort.[4]

What can the leaders of a business do to develop a sense of competitive urgency? In addition to their alertness to external forces at work, here are the chief characteristics of competitive top-management executives as I have observed them in action:

1. The competitive executive gets on with it. He treats time as his most valuable commodity and paces himself accordingly. He does not "fiddle around." At the same time, he works with calm purposefulness, rather than frantic haste.

2. The competitive executive works with zest. Typically, he works harder and more effectively than his subordinates. He sets a good example in work habits, not for the sake of setting an example but because he has a real zest for his job.

3. The competitive executive is decisive. After getting the

facts and thinking the problem or decision through, he makes a considered decision. He recognizes that he will make mistakes, but he knows that his competitors will, too; and he prefers risk of error to unnecessary delay. He knows he can safely be wrong part of the time, provided he keeps alert to opportunities for correcting errors.

I recall an executive who habitually made instant decisions that were not always sound. In talking with him, I discovered that just after graduating from college, he had spent a year as a minor-league baseball umpire. So he fell into the habit of making business decisions with nearly the same speed. Once aware of this, he realized that an executive—unlike an umpire—has an opportunity to gather and consider facts, to change his mind, and to correct his mistakes. So he began taking a little longer to think decisions through—and raised his batting average considerably.

4. The competitive executive seizes and exploits opportunities. He is more interested in building on strength than in shoring up weaknesses. He devotes more time to building his own company's position than to countering competitive moves. Therefore, a system for managing appeals to him.

5. The competitive executive seeks out and faces up to problems. He knows that the passage of time usually makes a tough problem even harder to solve. But when it cannot be solved immediately, he turns to developing company strengths and works around the problem while waiting for a better time to solve it.

6. The competitive executive does not shrink from difficult personnel decisions. He knows that unless poor performance can be overcome (as it often can), it is fairer to the company and the individual to remove him sooner rather than later. But the competitive executive is fair and not ruthless. He knows a management system will not be effective unless it facilitates fair and sound decisions affecting people.

Fair decisions concerning people are often received surprisingly well even by the person who is adversely affected. I recall the case of the leading salesman of a large industrial products company who spent much of his time at race tracks. Because of the large orders the marketing director thought the salesman controlled, for many years no action was taken to replace him. When a new marketing executive finally dismissed him, the salesman said he wondered why the action had not been taken long before. Of course, customer respect for the company increased, and no orders were lost.

7. The competitive executive focuses on increasing the company's share-of-market at a profit. His every action is directed toward building a stronger competitive position for the long term; but he takes the action now.

These are some of the characteristics of the executive who possesses a sense of competitive urgency. This incessant drive "to get on with it *now*" is necessary to succeed in our competitive profit-and-loss economy. More than management techniques, it makes our system the best means yet discovered for fulfilling people's material wants and needs profitably and for providing the psychic benefits of work itself. But that drive can be made more purposeful and effective by a management system. In turn, a management system helps develop a sense of competitive urgency. The interaction increases the likelihood of success for any enterprise.

Developing a Company Philosophy

In discussing the need for developing a company philosophy, rather than just letting it happen, I have selected from successful company experience just five common elements that make a good philosophical foundation for any business. To them, the management of any company or division can add other beliefs that should guide the organization. If they are to be a real part of the philosophy, however, these beliefs should be basic enough to become overriding guidelines to action.

Even without planning or specific effort, any company will gradually develop a philosophy as people observe and learn through trial and error "the way we do things around here." However, it is my conviction that a positive program by top management to build or reshape a sound fundamental philosophy should be the underlying and overriding component of the company's system of management.

Whatever beliefs top management wants to build into its philosophy must, of course, be demonstrated in practice if they are to take firm root in the minds of people throughout the organization. But to make the guidelines really operative, something more is needed than the power of example. Executives and supervisors at all levels should articulate the company philosophy, relate it to actual situations and problems at hand, and point out to subordinates where their actions square, or fail to square, with the beliefs of the organization. It is through this kind of leadership that a company philosophy for success can be most soundly and securely built.

Deeply and widely held beliefs in "the way we do things around here" provide a solid foundation on which to erect a programmed management system. And these beliefs interact with other system components to give them strength and to gain strength from them. This is especially true of the next component I discuss: strategic planning.

3

Strategic Planning: Shaping the Destiny and Competitive Cutting Edge of the Business

At a Sunday brunch in 1961, I was introduced to a man just back from London who was bubbling with enthusiasm about an English brand of stainless steel razor blades. After telling me how sharp they were and how long they lasted, he took a Wilkinson Sword stainless steel blade from his pocket and insisted that I try it. When I used the blade, I found the enthusiast's claims were, if anything, too modest.

A few weeks later, when I was in London, I went into a chemist's shop and asked for a package of Wilkinson blades. Rather condescendingly, the clerk informed me that they were out of stock. As I later learned from my English associates, even regular customers could rarely buy them. London executives, in fact, were sending their secretaries out to scour the chemists' shops in the hope of coming on a package occasionally.

Clearly this was a business phenomenon that was worth looking into. The reason for the success of the Wilkinson blade was not difficult to determine—its superiority in performance over any other on the market was so evident to the user that demand had simply outrun supply. Since then much has been written about the success of both the blade and the company. The dramatic story of how Wilkinson, as David, successfully fought Gillette, Goliath of the blade market, is now business history.

I intend no play on words in using the case of a razor blade to illustrate the ways that a company can shape its destiny and its competitive "cutting edge." The right course and a sharp competitive cutting edge for any business must begin with strategic planning of some sort, whether it be formal or so informal that it is done by default.

Nature and Phases of the Planning Process

Since strategic planning is only one phase of a company's total planning process, let us first get a common understanding of the whole process. In nontechnical terms, planning is decision making: deciding what to do, how to do it, and at what speed and cost to do it. Every person is constantly making such decisions in his daily living.

Down through the ages man has sought to gain understanding of the forces at work in his environment—and, with the aid of this understanding, to shield himself from the negative forces and to capitalize on the favorable ones. In a very real sense, therefore, the individual attains his chosen destiny to the degree that he understands and successfully copes with the forces at work in his environment. Failure and frustration are almost certain if he allows himself, consciously or subconsciously, to drift with the tides around him.

Much the same is true of business planning. The management either lets the business drift with the tides of its environment—or, through established management processes, seeks to control the destiny of the enterprise. Making decisions about the destiny of a business, however, is a much more complex process. Decisions on the use of many resources must be made by many people; and, of course, the plans must be carried out by many people. Therefore, some formality in assessing the environment and planning how to cope with it is obviously desirable if not essential.

Since people in a business must act, planning—formal or informal—is bound to take place. If it is not done formally and systematically, the creative thinking necessary for effective planning will be done hastily and half-consciously, under the pressure of daily events, as operating decisions are made. If overall plans are not made and communicated in an organized, systematic manner, then each department and section head will simply tell his people what he believes they should do, based on his personal understanding of objectives, goals, strategy, policies, and the budget. The multitude of informal planning decisions made in this fashion jell into an overall company or division plan. Many companies are managed that way and do quite well.

During the past decade, however, there has been an upsurge in determination to reduce corporate drift and to manage the destiny of the business by coping more effectively with forces at work in the environment. As a consequence, most U.S. companies have developed some degree of formalized planning. The results range from rudimentary financial plans to comprehensive strategic and operating plans that cover every activity in the business. In fact, this formalization has been carried to extremes in a few companies. One large durable goods manufacturer, for example, has more than 200 staff people engaged in developing and analyzing annual operating plans.

My observations convince me, however, that in most companies planning is still underdeveloped as a managing process. Indeed, better planning is still one of the new frontiers of better managing. Only recently has it received much attention from operating executives and students of management, and little standard practice has yet crystallized. What I have to say on the subject, therefore, reflects chiefly my own thinking and experience and that of my colleagues.

Consider one further parallel between planning by the individual and planning by the management of a business. In deciding how to work out his destiny, the individual can seek advice from his parents, teachers, spouse, minister, and friends—but only he can make the decisions about himself. So it is in business. Responsible line executives can seek advice from staff, subordinates, consultants, and executives in other companies. But only the line executive can make the decision. A planning staff can and should help the responsible line executive, but only he can decide.

As a rule, planning is left too much to the staff. They can only gather and analyze information and develop and recommend alternatives. If the line fails to get involved, if it fails to make decisions on the basis of these recommendations, then the staff turns to paper work and fruitless projections. This leads to staff frustration and line exasperation. Finally, the line decides that staff overhead is too heavy and cuts it back. The planning function suffers a setback—but only because the line has not done its job properly.

Each of the company's "businesses"—that is, each discrete set of products or services that combine naturally to seek user favor—calls for separate planning. Planning should also be done at the corporate level for the company as a whole, independent of the planning for each separate business. Thus, sound planning is *over-all* planning for each business and for the total company. Indeed, one of the great advantages of the proposed approach to planning is that it requires the top-management executives of the company and each division—at least annually —to think deeply, analytically, and creatively about each business and about the company as a whole, facing up to problems and deciding what to do about opportunities.

The value of such planning was well summarized by Harold Blancke, chairman of Celanese Corporation, in introducing a special issue of the *Celanese World* devoted entirely to planning at Celanese:

> Planning is so important today that it occupies a major part of the time of some of the most respected men in business—and in Celanese. Planning allows us to master change. Planning forces us to organize our expectations and develop a program to bring them about. It is a most effective way to draw out the best in all of us—our best thinking, our best interests and aims— and to enable us to develop the most efficient way of achieving our maximum growth.
>
> Long-range planning enabled Celanese to become the first chemical company to organize its major activities along completely international lines. It enabled us to launch ourselves into three entirely new and yet related fields of business in less than a year, and to increase our 1965 sales to more than $2\frac{1}{2}$ times our 1961 figure.
>
> Planning is the intellectual arm of organized growth. It is the prologue to tomorrow. And yet it is not the rarefied activity of a few people—it is really the business of all of us. . . . If Celanese is to continue to thrive and prosper, our planning activities must continue to lead the way, for careful and thorough planning is one vital key to the future of Celanese.[1]

The major changes in Celanese to which Mr. Blancke refers began with strategic planning—the first phase of the total planning process.

The Planning Spectrum

The total planning process is a continuum. It consists of determining objectives, establishing goals tied to objectives, developing strategy for achieving goals, developing programs or broad plans for carrying out strategy, and developing more detailed operational plans for carrying out the programs. The very nature of planning makes it difficult to divide the total process into phases for analysis and systemizing. One type of planning shades off into another like the colors of a spectrum, and determining where to make the separation is like trying to decide where the red in the spectrum shades into the orange.

Therefore, the breakdown of the planning cycle into phases and the procedures for planning will differ from company to company. However, since any planning system must involve many people at all levels, the procedures must be simple enough so they can be communicated broadly throughout the company. In most cases this can best be done by spelling out the procedures clearly in an understandable what-to-do and how-to-do-it guide or manual.

In discussing the planning process, I do not deal with planning procedure in any depth. My purpose is simply to define and describe this powerful management tool and show in specific terms, and through case examples, how any management can use it in a practical, workable manner. Each company must decide for itself how to divide the planning process and how to fit it procedurally into the most convenient planning cycle.

The best recent experience shows the conceptual and practical value of breaking the planning process into three closely related phases:

■ *Strategic planning,* which is discussed in this chapter, includes determination of company, division, and business objectives; establishment of major goals tied to objectives; and development of strategies for achieving those goals. In a multibusiness company, strategic planning should be conducted on three separate levels: the *business, division,* and *corporate.*

Strategic planning at the corporate level, which is often neglected as an element of the planning effort, requires top corporate management to make the tough decisions required for the most profitable allocation of the corporation's total human, financial, and technical resources. These decisions are based on objectives and strategy established for the total company in the light of the outlook for each individual business and division and the opportunities for the company as a whole. The objectives and strategies—i.e., the strategic plans—for each business and for the total company should be put in writing to guide the subsequent phases of the planning process.

■ *Management programming,* which is discussed in Chapter 7, is the central phase of planning. The management program, which ordinarily has a 2- to 6-year time focus, translates the strategic plans into integrated sets of qualitative and quantitative plans for each business and division, readily convertible into the operational plans on which budgets are based. The written management program, with its supporting data, is the heart of the planning process. Besides providing a factual basis for corporate strategic planning, it helps to test existing strategic plans for each business and point up the need for developing new ones.

■ *Operational planning* (also discussed in Chapter 7) covers the actual conversion of management programs into the specific annual plans that incorporate functional work assignments and schedules and that provide the basis for the annual operating budget and any capital budgets.

In a divisionalized business, strategic planning for the total company is done by top-management executives at corporate headquarters under the leadership of the corporate chief executive, who is finally responsible. In a multidivisional business, where strategy is carried out by the divisions, management programming is not done at the corporate level. Instead, strategic planning and the management programming for each division are done by division top management, under the leadership of the division chief executive. Operational planning is done by division and appropriate lower level executives and approved by top corporate management.

As we will see in Chapter 7, management programming and operational planning are usually done at the same time. Simply because of the spectrum-like character of the planning process, they are bound to overlap. But I believe that better results are likely if these two stages are set up separately and sequentially, even though in practice they will be going on pretty much together.

Although the same information can be used for both strategic planning and management programming purposes, I believe in putting separate emphasis on strategic planning. In fact, it is because the concept of strategic planning is so important to profitable, dynamic growth that I discuss it early in the book, separating it by several chapters from the more detailed discussion of the balance of the planning process in Chapter 7.

Nature of Strategic Planning

Top managements that are committed to systematic strategic planning are highly successful, I have observed, because they come to think deeply, creatively, and continuously in terms of this question: "What are we trying to do—and how can we do it most profitably in the face of competition?" Strategic thinking compels constant attention to the fundamental factors controlling success. This gives a company a sharp competitive cutting edge—and keeps it sharp by focusing on accomplishments, performance, and results.

I do not contend that creative thinking can be proceduralized. Brilliant flashes of inspiration have always paid off handsomely in every field of endeavor, and they are not likely to be superseded by systematized, methodical thinking. But I do contend that an organized approach to the total planning process and especially to strategic thinking can enable men, without the benefit of inspiration, to make solid contributions that would otherwise be lost. In other words, I believe that any management can pull itself up significantly by its own thought-bootstraps through attention to strategic planning.

An organized approach to this system component will also make it easier for a management to contend better with competition and with the enormous and increasing complexities of the business environment resulting from technological, political, and social change.

The term "strategy," of course, comes from military science and relates to generalship and maneuver. In this sense, a dictionary definition is "the science and art of employing the political, economic, psychological, and military forces of a nation or group of nations to afford the maximum support to adopted policies in peace or war." This military definition can be converted to business terms: Business strategy is the science and art of deploying all the resources of the business (men, materials, money, and management) in achieving established objectives and goals successfully (i.e., more profitably) in the face of competition.

This definition will be a more useful guide to strategic thinking if two points made previously are kept in mind. First, strategic planning includes the setting of objectives and goals as well as the development of strategy itself. Second, corporate success is measured by growth in sales, volume, share-of-market, and net profit; satisfactory rate of return on investment; and continuity of effective management. Strategy should be designed accordingly.

In developing a really useful understanding of strategic

thinking, it may be helpful to bear in mind this dictionary definition of "strategic": "Of great or vital importance within an integrated whole or to the taking place of a planned or unplanned occurrence." Translating that from military to business terms, and getting away from dictionary jargon, we have: Strategic thinking about a business concerns fundamental plans for dealing with internal developments and external forces that affect the long-term success of the business as an integrated whole. Or, more briefly, *the strategic thinker is concerned with fundamental issues affecting the long-term success of the business as an integrated whole.*

Strategic-thinking managers train themselves to recognize the *relationship* and *significance* of specific developments to the long-term success of the business as a whole, and to develop plans and policies for coping with and capitalizing on those developments. Since I cannot over-emphasize the importance of this point, let me put it another way: The strategic thinker learns to identify significant specific developments and then modifies one or more system components—objectives, strategy, management program, operational plans, policy, organization structure, etc. —so as to cope with or capitalize on these developments.

Tactics, in the military sense, are lesser plans for carrying out strategy. The dictionary defines "tactical" as "involving actions or means of less magnitude than those of strategy . . . or relative to small-scale actions serving a larger purpose . . . or carried out with only a limited end in view." This concept, too, is useful in business. Tactics, which support strategy just as goals support objectives, are taken up in Chapter 7 as part of management programming and operational planning.

The nature of *strategic* planning can be further illuminated by briefly considering long-range planning, forecasting, and budgeting.

  ▪ *Long-range planning:* So-called long-range planning,

which is frequently regarded as synonymous with strategic planning, has recently attained considerable popularity. It is a beguiling concept and term. Most top-management executives have a guilty feeling that they are too much occupied with day-to-day decision making. Establishing a "long-range planning" staff sounds dynamic and forward-looking, and at least it relieves the guilty feeling. But to me the term is confusing because *long-range* refers to the time dimension rather than to the *type* of planning.

Unfortunately, too, "long-range" plans have typically taken the form of relatively useless profit projections, often extending as far as 10 years ahead. Usually these plans involve enormous amounts of paper work and limited amounts of strategic thinking. Many tend to assume that the present strategy will continue unchanged. Instead of dealing with fundamentals, challenging present strategy, and developing various alternatives and their respective profit implications or consequences, they merely attempt to portray the future. And since no one can really foresee what is going to happen 10 or even 7 years ahead, such long-term profit projections are easily dismissed as "blue-sky," thus tending to discredit the whole planning process.

One company I know, for example, had a "long-range planning" program that annually produced, by dint of monumental efforts, a 10-year profit projection. In this particular business, everyone recognized that to project profits realistically for 2 years ahead was impossible. Understandably, "long-range planning" got a bad name—and later, in attempting to install a real strategic planning effort, management found that it had to cut through a fog of misunderstanding and overcome determined resistance.

No, *long-range* planning and *strategic* planning are not synonymous, because strategic planning is not necessarily long range. Some strategic plans—e.g., plans for the acquisition, sale, or liquidation of a business—can be carried out in a few months. However, since objectives tend to be enduring and since basic strategy seldom changes overnight, strategic planning usually does quite properly have a long-range focus.

In point of fact, strategy is concerned more with *how* objectives and goals can be achieved rather than *when*, although the time it will take to carry out alternate strategies necessarily affects their relative attractiveness. Under the proposed approach to planning, management programs are concerned with an intermediate range of time and operational plans with short-term specific time schedules.

For these reasons, I believe that the term "strategic planning" is preferable to "long-range planning." The latter may, of course, be used as a synonym for strategic planning, but I prefer *strategic* because it emphasizes the nature of the planning rather than the time period. However, if an executive group prefers *"long-range strategic planning,"* the slight inaccuracy in this lengthier term is not significant.

■ *Forecasting:* Perhaps because forecasts—or estimates of what will happen—play an important part in developing strategic plans, forecasting frequently gets confused with strategic planning. The two procedures are, however, quite different. Forecasting has a role in *all* phases of planning, but comes into greater play as the planning process approaches the operational end of the spectrum.

■ *Budgeting:* An operating budget is the translation of operational plans into income, costs, expenses, and profits for a specified period—usually a year. Budgeting is neither forecasting nor strategic planning, though it usually draws on both. In preparing a budget, sales volume must either be forecast or assumed, and some attention must be given to strategy, if only to existing strategy. The planning incidental to preparing a budget is often regarded as adequate. However, strategies and management programs developed during the budgeting process are unlikely to produce many competitive breakthroughs.

The nature and power of strategic planning can be further illuminated by considering the field of government, where the same basic principles apply. Speaking at Amherst College, former Secretary of State Dean Acheson said:

> What, then, is the sound approach to questions of foreign policy? I suggest that it is what we might call the strategic approach—to consider various courses of action from the point of view of their bearing upon major objectives.[2]

The power of strategic thinking as a guide to action is shown by President Lincoln's approach to the Civil War. In response to a question from editor Horace Greeley, Lincoln wrote in 1862:

> My paramount object in this struggle *is* to save the Union, and is *not* either to save or destroy slavery. If I could save the Union without freeing *any* slave, I would do it, and if I could save it by freeing all the slaves, I would do it; and if I could do it by freeing some and leaving others alone, I would also do that. What I do about slavery and the colored race, I do because I believe it helps to save the Union; and what I forebear, I forebear because I do *not* believe it would help to save the Union. [Italics are Lincoln's.] [3]

The value of strategic planning is recognized in great educational institutions. In Yale University's 1964–1965 annual report, President Kingman Brewster, Jr., calls education "our primary mission." Under the heading "Perspective for Planning," he writes:

> Your trustees, the President and Fellows of the Yale Corporation, need a strategy of ends and means if they are to give Yale direction and are to appraise Yale's course from month to month and from year to year. . . .

One impetus for developing a strategy is the need for priorities by which to ration scarce resources. . . .

Another consideration which must pervade any strategic thinking is a continuous examination of our inherent and inherited comparative advantages and disadvantages. . . .

Educational wisdom and parsimony alike compel attention to the obvious fact that we can do some things . . . better than, or not as well as, others do them. . . .

These ways of thinking . . . describe the proper cast of mind for those who are responsible for the direction of the University as a whole. [Italics supplied.]

Again, the Harvard Business School seeks students with the highest potential as business leaders, in order to make the best use of its scarce resources—faculty, facilities, and money. Thus, even though the school is already swamped with applications, the strategy of Dean George P. Baker calls for an aggressive student recruiting program.

These examples from government and education show that strategic planning is concerned chiefly with adjusting the organization to its environment, solving basic problems, coping with limitations, capitalizing on inherent and developed advantages, and seizing major new opportunities.

The same principles apply in business, as Mr. Sloan makes clear in *My Years with General Motors*. Again, the American Telephone & Telegraph Company has been strategically managed almost throughout its history, and during Frederick Kappel's administration several new strategic concepts have given new dynamism to the business. Du Pont, after World War I, made strategic decisions to convert the company from an explosives business to what is now the world's largest and most successful chemical business.

But the need for strategic planning, as examples will show, is not confined to organizations on the grand scale of governments, universities, or great national corporations. Relatively speaking, it is just as powerful an instrument for the independent local grocer. And it is at least as necessary. Indeed, in meeting the competition of corporate food chains, the local grocer *must* do strategic planning or perish.

Approach to Strategic Planning

In the words of Kingman Brewster, strategic planning is concerned with "ways of thinking" about the direction an organization is taking. I believe that strategic planning about the direction a business is taking can be done most systematically and effectively if these steps are taken:

1. Fix accountability for strategic planning in line executives, with the chief executive primarily responsible.

2. Divide strategic planning into levels; develop plans for each separate business; and establish a grand design for each division and for the company as a whole—i.e., the objectives and strategy covering all of the individual businesses included in the division and the company.

3. Define each kind of business in which the company is engaged, and set its objectives and goals separately.

4. Divide strategic thinking and planning for each kind of business into three interrelated phases:

- User (or product/market) strategy: how to serve selected market segments of users continuously better—and always better than competitors
- Profit strategy: how to maximize profits by exploiting the profit economics of the business
- Executive manpower strategy: how to attract, retain, and develop capable people—especially the high-talent, high-caliber manpower needed for continuity of effective management.

This division of strategic planning and thinking gears it to the three measures of corporate success. Each separate strategy requires a somewhat different type of thinking and facts, yet each can be integrated with the others without much difficulty. Together they constitute *a way of thinking* about business strategy.

5. Finally, provide an appropriate staff to assist the line executives in their planning work.

Throughout the entire planning process, of course, the factfounded approach should be employed. Overlooking or disregarding facts of importance can be costly or fatal. Moreover, the factual approach to planning produces practical and realistic rather than "blue-sky" results. At the same time, all present major assumptions about the business should be challenged, and imaginative alternatives examined without bias.

Responsibility for Planning

The crucial role of the chief executive in strategic planning is pointed up by another dictionary definition of strategy: "The science and art of military command exercised to meet the enemy in combat under advantageous conditions." Since "command" starts at the top in any organization, the chief executive of a business, division, or company must be responsible for its strategy.

Of course, the grand design (i.e., makeup by businesses) and other major strategic plans of the company as a whole should be approved by the board of directors; and divisional chief executives will need more detailed approvals from corporate top management. But any chief executive must decide or recommend the strategy for his organization, and that responsibility cannot be delegated. It is a *command* decision.

The chief executive, of course, must have help in developing strategic plans. For best results, I believe he should utilize an informal "cabinet" of line managers who do serious thinking, consciously and collectively, about objectives, goals, and strategy. The group will usually be made up of half a dozen executives who report to the chief executive, and perhaps a few others—no more than 10 in all.

Periodically—once a year, unless some major development calls for an earlier strategic reassessment—the chief executive should meet with his "cabinet" for a deep examination of the business, its outlook and competitive position. This examination should probably be made just before the combined preparation of the management program and operating plan (as discussed in Chapter 7). It should take place away from the pressure of daily events—perhaps even away from company or division offices. And it should involve separate review of user, profit, and manpower strategies.

In a large company or division, the "cabinet" should be joined by the director of corporate (or divisional) planning—a staff executive who, as we will see, is responsible for staff help on all phases of planning. Before the group thinking begins, he and his staff should gather facts and develop alternate strategies for consideration. But the actual planning, since it is decision making, must be done by the line; direct participation of line executives is the key to success. When line and staff work out plans together in a systematic and organized way, they stimulate each other's thinking—often with surprising results.

Direct involvement of the chief executive on a command basis is important in business for another reason: the great resistance to change that exists in every large organization. Even the most successful companies contain innumerable points of resistance to change: outmoded organization structures, policies, and procedures; personnel inadequacies both in capabilities and number; inadequate communications; lack of understanding;

established patterns of habit; vested interests; and political ambitions.

Since changes in strategic plans typically involve fundamental operational changes, the authority and leadership of the chief executive are usually essential to successful execution. As will appear from later case examples, effective strategic planning is often not so much a matter of tactical ingenuity as it is of timing and effective action. (A well-designed and well-established system of management will lessen resistance to change and step up effective action.)

Levels of Strategic Planning

The terms *strategic planning* and *corporate planning* are frequently thought to apply solely to entering new businesses—that is, to diversifying by acquisition or merger or through the development of new products or services. Because such decisions so obviously relate to the grand design (makeup) of the company, they do call for careful strategic planning; but strategic planning, properly understood, is by no means confined to such moves.

In most companies, extensive opportunities for increasing success through better planning, including strategic planning, exist in each separate "business"—i.e., each discrete set of products or services that compete for user favor. A company or even a division may comprise several such businesses. Maximizing the total success of the company requires effective strategic planning for each separate business—as well as planning at the corporate level, where the grand design of a diversified company is shaped.

Even developing the grand design, however, requires strategic thinking about each separate business the company might enter, either by marketing new products of its own or by acquiring an existing company. The building blocks of the various businesses should be fitted together in the grand design of the total enterprise. Each block should have its own sound strategic plans. Except in conglomerate companies, each should provide strategic support for the others.

Industry Outlook and Competitive Position

As background for setting objectives and goals and for developing user, profit, and manpower strategies, every corporate and division management should make a searching, factual analysis of the profit outlook in its industry or industries, and the competitive position of the company and division in each. The quality and depth of this analysis will largely determine the success of the whole planning process.

The industry analysis should emphasize trends rather than current position alone. It should be broad enough and deep enough to take into account such factors as:

- Trends in volume, costs, prices, and return on investment compared with other industries
- Industry profit economics: key factors determining profits such as volume, materials, labor, capital investment, market penetration, and dealer strength
- Ease of entry into the industry, including capital investment
- Relationship between current and future demand and manufacturing capacity, and its probable effects on prices and profits.

In turn, the analysis of the company's competitive position should fully evaluate the trends in the company's volume and share-of-market—and provide detailed, concrete information on over-all competitive strengths and weaknesses. The specific strengths and weaknesses of each principal product group should be identified and analyzed in terms of each major market or market segment. Important new entries into each market should be identified and their effects assessed.

Equipped with a fundamental and factual assessment of these environmental and competitive factors, the top executives of the most successful companies and divisions keep alert to changes that may affect either the industry or the company position in it. Since they are determined to cope successfully with the business environment, not drift with the tides of change, these leaders constantly seek to identify the forces at work and evaluate the impact of each. They examine alternatives imaginatively, without bias in favor of existing plans. And, typically, they see to it that this analysis is reduced to a written document—not a lengthy, general treatise but a crisp, quantitative and qualitative summary of alternatives and factors that need to be considered in making the strategic decisions that will govern corporate success.

Objectives

If asked to state the objective of his company, the typical chief executive would probably say with some feeling, "To make a profit!"

It is true, of course, that a company *must* make a profit to stay in business, and it must make a satisfactory rate of profit in order to be successful. The notion that profit is the objective of a business is therefore beguiling—but it is often both dangerous and self-defeating. I believe that the managers of any business will make better strategic decisions if they think of profit as a reward for serving users well—not so much an objective in itself as a yardstick of managerial effectiveness in achieving other objectives.

Better strategic thinking and decision making will result, I suggest, if the objectives of the company are conceived in terms of offering products or services of such value to the user as to *entitle* the company to expanding volume and profits. The distinction may sound academic, but it is both real and useful. I believe that this concept of profits will foster more effective thinking about user, profit, and manpower strategies.

It is well to keep in mind that in a competitive economy, profits must be *earned*. They are thus a basic measure of the relative competitive value of a company's contribution to users, distributors, employees, and the public. And it is only by maximizing that contribution that a company can maximize its profits over the long term. As one leading executive with whom I discussed this distinction said, "Oh, I see: Concentrate on things that produce profit rather than on profit itself."

President Calvin Coolidge put it this way:

> No enterprise can exist for itself alone. It ministers to some great need, it performs some great service, not for itself, but for others; or failing therein, it ceases to be profitable and ceases to exist.

More recently, Gerald L. Phillippe, chairman of the board of General Electric Company, expressed the same notion well in a speech entitled "The Public Be Served":

> As businessmen became more sophisticated in marketing and business decisions, we have learned anew that the royal road to business success is to serve the changing wants and needs of the public just as faithfully as we can. It is more profitable—as well as more responsible, socially—to find out what people want and need, and set up to serve them efficiently.[4]

Perhaps you will feel that using profit as a measure instead of an objective is a distinction without a difference. Maybe so. But I believe it is a useful distinction to guide the thinking of top managers in developing strategy—particularly user strategy.

The objectives of a company or division—or its "mission," if the more inspirational synonym is preferred—should be set in broad, enduring terms that will focus the attention of everyone on "what we are trying to do" or "the kind of business we want to have." The objectives or mission should define how the organization will serve people, and hence should be expressed in service terms.

Du Pont meets these criteria with its slogan, "Better things for better living through chemistry." The objectives and strategy reflected in that slogan have kept Du Pont dynamic and growing within the field of chemistry, based on sound user strategy. Another excellent statement of objectives is found in the 1965 annual report of International Business Machines Corporation:

> Our business is the creation of machines and methods to help find solutions to the increasingly complex problems of business, government, science, space exploration, education, medicine, and nearly every other area of human endeavor.

An objective is enduring, timeless, never fully achieved. Yet to guide and motivate people, a statement of objectives should be definitive. Du Pont and IBM both define their objectives in terms of serving others, and thus their statements have an inspirational value for the company people who must achieve them.

The nature of objectives will be more fully illustrated in case examples further on. First, however, something should be said about one universal company objective: growth. Obviously, the volume, share-of-market, and profit measures of corporate success all require that the organization grow. Somewhat less obvious, but even more important in the long run, is the fact that growth is necessary to attract and hold the able people needed for continuity of effective management—our third measure of corporate success. Without growth to provide opportunities for advancement, as well as increased compensation, capable executive talent is hard to attract. Able people will leave while the less competent stay on, thus starting a blight that can lead to the extinction of the business.

The full significance of this reason for growth is too frequently overlooked in developing and applying a system of management. Moreover, many top managements fail to take full advantage of the growth objective in motivating people through internal communications. By convincing all levels of management that growth is an objective vital to long-term survival, top managers can help develop the will to manage in junior executives, improve individual performance, and build esprit. That is the multiplier effect of the system at work. In short, the importance of growth as a basic ingredient in user, profit, and manpower strategies should make it a conscious and articulated objective of every business.

The advisability of distinguishing between objectives and goals has been mentioned earlier. Goals and subgoals are specific targets for planning and action. Goals, as subobjectives, are tied to objectives; and subgoals are tied to goals. Goals and subgoals are targets quantified in value and/or time, and should be realistically attainable. Thus, a profit goal may be a specific amount for a particular period. Or a more permanent goal may be set in terms of return on investment. Since goals are guides in developing management programs and operating plans, they are discussed in more detail in Chapter 7.

User Strategy

With corporate and division objectives established, strategic planning begins with user, or product/market, strategy. This means finding ways to serve users that will expand volume and share-of-market and so help to increase profits.

User strategy is well described in an article by J. W. Keener, president of B. F. Goodrich:

> This means that everything that business does must be pointed to the market. It means that every business function must be directed toward and be in tune with the market. Research and development, production, finance and control, personnel, all and more, must at all times watch what the market does.[5]

Later in the article Mr. Keener speaks of "users," a term I prefer to "market." In any case, he is right on target.

All intermediaries (distributors, dealers, retailers, etc.) should also be considered, of course, when developing user strategy. In fact, the most effective user strategy is designed for everyone who makes or influences the buying decision. An early step in developing strategy, therefore, is to determine who makes and/or influences the buying decision. That is part of the factual raw material of user strategy.

The main focus of user strategy should be on the ultimate user, because ordinarily he will make or strongly influence the buying decision. If possible, however, strategic appeals should also be developed for every intermediary. Sometimes—as when the product lacks distinctiveness and must be sold on a commodity basis—user strategy will rest almost exclusively on these strategic appeals to intermediaries. Ideally, however, user strategy should *start* with the user and work back.

The best user strategy, I believe, will result from concentrating fact-gathering and thinking on four strategic elements: (1) product performance, (2) service, (3) brand acceptance, and (4) price.

If the user does not recognize authentic reasons for buying

your product's particular combination of performance, service, and brand acceptance, then you will have to price it lower. Put another way, competitive price is simply a reflection of the relative combined competitive strength of product performance, service, and brand acceptance—your particular *package* of user values. Facts should be gathered and strategic plans designed to maximize the competitive attractiveness of that *package* so it may be priced accordingly. That is why I believe that marketing should generally provide the competitive cutting edge of the business.

Let's consider each of these four strategic elements briefly, using case examples to show how they can serve as guides for strategic thinking in developing a user, or product/market, strategy:

1. *Product performance:* What was the secret of Wilkinson Sword stainless steel razor blades? How could a newcomer like Wilkinson, selling a higher-priced product with little advertising support, carve out a sizable share of a market dominated by Gillette? The answer: superior product performance that the user could easily detect for himself. Wilkinson's strategy was clearly user-focused. And Gillette struck back with a user-focused strategy—improving the performance of its own blades and developing an entirely new product that combines the razor and blade.

The Wilkinson strategy of superior product performance had two aspects. First, product performance actually *was* superior by laboratory test. Second, that superiority was easily recognized by the user. In fact, it was so striking that at first word of mouth took the place of paid advertising.

In the ladies' field, nylon stockings made an even more dramatic product performance entry into the market. In the industrial field, the fluorescent lamp was the counterpart of stainless steel razor blades and nylon stockings. All these products served users better—obviously better. Substantial profits came as a by-product.

This strategic concept is well expressed in the Du Pont slogan: "Better things for better living through chemistry." The extraordinary return on investment that Du Pont has achieved over the years largely results from management's ability to make that slogan come true in the form of a constant flow of dramatically better new products: automobile finishes, cellophane, nylon, Dacron, and Corfam, to name just a few. The superior performance of all these products could be recognized by the user. The automobile finish was also better for an intermediary, the auto manufacturer: By drying much faster, it enabled him to substantially reduce work-in-process inventories.

Basically, the user buys your product because it will do more for him than competitive products. That is, it gives him or her more tangible benefits (a more comfortable shave), intangible satisfactions (better-looking legs), and/or greater value (longer-lasting blades; stockings that look good and wear well).

Product performance is a broad concept. It is not confined to tangible features that demonstrably provide an edge over competitors in functional performance or cost. Fashion, style, and prestige come into play. The prestige perfume "performs" better than unknown brands, even though it may smell no better to most people. Superior performance may even be a matter of the package, e.g., the easy-open can.

Service, brand acceptance, and price aside, the reasons why users can be brought to prefer your product are legion. And the best user strategy focuses first—factually, consistently, resolutely, and imaginatively—on superior product performance for the user. That is the best way to build values that entitle the business to higher profits. The margin of superiority need not be great, but in a competitive economy it must be authentic.

The central importance of the product in strategic planning is well summarized in Mr. Keener's article:

> Everything starts with the needs and wants of the ultimate user of a product. The nature of the product—its specifications, its style, its color, its size, its quality, its price—all must be suited to what the ultimate user thinks he needs and wants. Those who are in tune with this marketing fundamental are those who will be the growth leaders in the coming decade.

Testifying before a Senate subcommittee in 1956, Harlow Curtice, then president of GM, was asked whether the test of management effectiveness was ability to make a satisfactory return on investment. He said: "That is certainly it, but we have to do better than that because each year we must have something, either greater value or lower price, for the customer."

2. Service: The user may buy your product because you offer better service than competitors. This service advantage may take many forms. The product may simply be more convenient to purchase. Delivery may be prompter or more reliable. Standard products may be offered in smaller quantities or unusual combinations. To help the user apply, maintain, or conserve the product, technical service may be offered. The company may gain its edge over competitors by a policy of accepting returns without question.

Service strategy is frequently used for commodities and commodity-type industrial products. But superior service strengthens the strategy for consumer products, too. For example, both General Foods and Johnson & Johnson have developed warehouse and delivery systems that enable them to make quick and economical deliveries of bulk combinations of small quantities of individual products.

Unusual service has played an important part in the success of GM's Truck & Coach Division. A 1956 staff report to a Senate subcommittee studying the antitrust laws describes how GM achieved a major competitive advantage through a unique "group of trained specialists who could effectively and efficiently survey the total operation of a particular [customer] company and make sound and helpful recommendations to improve its overall efficiency." The Senate staff commented that "such a service to small operators, working with limited capital, in a field requiring considerable know-how, would be of tremendous value, particularly since it is obtainable without charge."

3. *Brand acceptance:* The user may prefer your products to those of competitors because he has more confidence in your company or your brand, based on experience with product performance or service. Thus, a woman may buy one refrigerator rather than another because a friend who owns the same brand says it hardly ever needs a service call.

Confidence in brand or company may come from advertising, provided product performance lives up to advertising claims. Thus, most consumers favor nationally advertised brands because they have come to recognize that national advertisers' quality and other performance claims can generally be trusted.

The point comes across in the same Senate staff report on GM quoted earlier. "In addition," it notes, "the vast consumer goodwill built up by General Motors over a considerable period of time as a result of this advertising investment, as well as a record of successful performance, provides the company with a definite advantage over smaller competitors which is not necessarily based upon considerations of quality, price, or service."

4. *Price:* To repeat: Unless you give the user authentic and recognizable performance, service, or brand-acceptance reasons for buying your product, then you must resort to lower price in order to offer competitive values that will command share-of-market at a profit. Lower prices, narrower gross profit margins, and lower return on investment are competitive penalties that any business must pay if it cannot develop a strategy that gives the user a more competitive package of values. Conversely, higher prices, wider gross profit margins, and higher return on investment are the rewards for planning a user strategy that produces a distinctive package of product performance, service, and/or brand acceptance.

User-focused strategic thinking and planning apply to all types of businesses. Commodities such as copper, cement, and cotton sell chiefly on a price basis because they have no other user strategy. Yet the strategic thinking of their managers is a constant quest for superiority of product performance, service, and/or brand acceptance. Aluminum companies have based their strategy on persuading users to replace other commodities with theirs by demonstrating its superior performance and/or value. Cement companies employ a service strategy in building storage terminals to provide better customer service at points distant from their plants.

In any company, the marketing function has primary responsibility for helping top line managers shape the destiny and competitive cutting edge of the business. Marketing managers should be the chief, though not the sole, suppliers of facts for user strategy. They should also have primary responsibility for developing the alternatives that the chief executive will consider in finally determining what user strategy to adopt.

Now let's examine some actual examples of how companies in a variety of businesses have developed effective user strategies.

■ *War in the automobile industry.* The familiar story of American Motors Corporation provides a dramatic example of how a "small" company in real financial difficulty managed to regain—at least for a time—a substantial position in a highly competitive industry dominated by a single company, General Motors, whose 1963 sales were $16.5 billion compared with AMC's $1.2 billion.

AMC was formed in 1954 through the merger of two ailing companies, Nash-Kelvinator Corporation and the Hudson Motor Car Company. At about that time the three leading automobile companies, moving to meet what they believed to be a demand for larger and more powerful cars, were obliged to raise their prices by $75 to $100 each year. This opened a gap into which AMC's smaller, less costly Rambler, along with some foreign makes, could move.

AMC management exploited this opportunity by agressively merchandising the virtues of a compact and economical car and attacking the "gas-guzzling dinosaurs" of its competitors. Between 1957 and 1960, Rambler sales rose steadily from about 120,000 to nearly 480,000, and the company's share-of-market soared from 1.7 percent to 7.1 percent. Annual profits averaged nearly $41 million between 1959 and 1963. As one observer put it, "The rise of American Motors was one of the biggest success stories of American business." [6] AMC management observed changes in the basis of the consumer buying decision, resulting from a growing interest in operating economy; noted small-car gaps in the product lines of competitors; and found that AMC's small car could be moved into this gap.

Although the big three automobile makers soon countered Rambler and the foreign cars with their own compacts, the case shows that competitive advantage against strong competition can be gained through user strategy that provides real and recognizable user advantage—and then lost or lessened when that advantage ceases or diminishes.

■ *Strategy in the container and carton industries.* Companies in the highly competitive corrugated and solid fiber shipping container and folding carton industries employ two basically different strategies. Those that are essentially in timber and paper businesses have integrated vertically by buying direct customers—shipping container and folding carton manufacturers. They generally regard these container and carton divisions simply as means for using up the paperboard and timber on which their profit is made. Thus, these companies have not focused their strategy on the ultimate user.

A contrasting strategy is followed by Container Corporation of America. Speaking to the New York Society of Security Analysts in 1963, President Leo H. Schoenhofen described it this way:

> Our business is packaging, and our strategy is to add maximum value to paperboard in the converting process in order to earn a maximum return on invested capital.
>
> The value added comes in the form of ingenious structural design, outstanding graphic design, and high-quality printing. Obviously, our customers don't ask us to add these values just so Container Corporation can earn a good return on investment. Our customers want sound structure and good graphics in their packaging because these things add up to more sales appeal and more consumer satisfaction. . . .
>
> Our emphasis has been on marketing services, as opposed to fully integrated operations. We are buyers of paperboard, pulp, and pulp wood over and above our own production or resources, thereby retaining flexibility of material used in our operations. Our partial integration has enabled us to run our mills to capacity and be somewhat selective in business booked. This has had a lot to do with the fact that our earnings of $1.72 per share were off only 6 percent from our peak year. . . .

While we are primarily in paper packaging, we are alert to any and all packaging materials which offer market and profit opportunities. Various materials are currently used in combination with paperboard as laminates or components. . . .

That this strategy works is indicated by Container Corporation's earning record. As many of you probably noticed, *Bankers Monthly Magazine* reported about a month ago that Container Corporation's return on capital in the 1956 to 1962 period was 10.1 percent compared with 7.8 percent for its six major competitors. . . .

The difference between these two strategies is great. One focuses on chewing up timber or keeping paper mills busy, while the other focuses on helping Container Corporation's direct purchasers sell more of *their* products to the ultimate users of those products, thus increasing their requirements for shipping containers and cartons.

The user-focused strategy has a substantially different impact on operations. Container Corporation has large staffs concerned with package design, packaging machinery development, and packaging research. Most of the companies that employ a raw-material-oriented strategy also carry on these same activities, but they are typically less extensive and are defensively oriented. In most industries, the record shows, a user-focused strategy pays best because it serves best.

■ *Strategy in fashion goods.* With fiscal 1964 sales of $88 million and profits of $7 million, Bobbie Brooks, Inc., is one of the largest and most successful manufacturers of women's dresses. Here is one of the keys to that success, as described by *The Wall Street Journal:*

The strategy is simple: Pick a target group—for Bobbie, girls aged 15 to 24. Study their clothing tastes as thoroughly as you can. Design specifically for them, aim promotion specifically at them, stage fashion shows exclusively for them. . . .

And sell to them in special "junior miss" departments, where-ever stores can be persuaded to set them up, so that a girl can select her clothes without wandering around the store lost in a crowd of older women shoppers.

But, in a field where many firms are too small to have any organized marketing strategy at all, this approach has made Bobbie something of an anomaly.[7]

This strategy has led the company to avoid fads, to develop distinctive distribution methods, and to concentrate on promoting direct to the ultimate user. In an industry marked by bitter competition, savage price cutting, and a staggering mortality rate, the success of Bobbie Brooks stands out. It underlines again the value of a *leadership* strategy that does not hesitate to depart from industry practices. And it shows how, by keeping all activities consistent with the established strategy, Bobbie Brooks has achieved a constancy of purpose that increases its consumer and retailer impact.

■ *Strategies in service businesses.* At the end of 1963, Merrill Lynch, Pierce, Fenner & Smith had about 150 offices in the United States, Canada, and overseas. Its customers numbered 500,000, up from 48,000 in 1940. Its income from operations in that year was $170 million (up from $9 million in 1942); it did more than 12 percent of the round-lot volume and nearly 20 percent of the odd-lot volume on the New York Stock Exchange (compared with 9.3 percent and 10.2 percent in 1942); it had $108 million in capital funds (up from $6 million in 1942), and net income of nearly $18 million (compared with $146,000 in 1942). In 1964—its fiftieth year—the firm made its fiftieth acquisition of another firm or office.

The strategic planning that produced this outstanding success record is based on the shrewd foresight of Charles Merrill, the founder. Long before others, he foresaw that the future of the securities business would depend less and less on wealthy investors, and more and more on multitudes of small stockholders.

His strategy was first set forth in 1940 in a "Statement of Policy" that begins, "The interests of our customers must come first." In explaining this policy, which appears on the back of each of Merrill Lynch's annual reports, the firm has said: [8]

> We claim no monopoly on this virtue, for the success of any broker depends primarily on his ability to satisfy his customers. Translated into a broker's daily operation, a basic policy like this means that there are no insiders, that he plays no favorites, that his opinions are not shaded by undisclosed self-interest. Decisions turn not on whether we can make money in a given transaction, but on whether it is to our customer's advantage. All our other policies are designed to give effect to this principle.

Under the leadership of the top-management team of Michael McCarthy and George J. Leness, these policies have been developed into a set of beliefs to guide employees in operating the business. In a field where the will to manage is minimal, Merrill Lynch clearly has an effective system of management to carry out the strategy and apply the principles that Mr. Merrill inaugurated. Mr. Merrill also had the foresight to bring Mr. McCarthy in from the chain store field, and Mr. McCarthy and Mr. Leness had the vision and determination to build an effective system of management.

It is no surprise, therefore, that the firm has prospered. It has had constancy of purpose, emanating from continuing conceptual and executive leadership at the top. These leaders have developed a system of management to carry their will to manage to thousands of employees in the firm's network of offices, and the system really guides the enterprise. An important component of the Merrill Lynch system is strategic planning, clearly expressed in writing as a guide to the thinking and actions of everyone in the firm. The leaders inspire and require adherence to the system and to the strategic plans they have developed.

A brief look at another field, publications, again illustrates the value of effective strategic planning in a service business. To my mind, the five publications that stand out most from their competitors are *The New York Times, Time, The New Yorker, The Wall Street Journal,* and *The Economist* of London. All five are the envy of their respective competitors—if indeed *The Wall Street Journal, The New Yorker,* and *The Economist* have any direct competitors.

Their great success illustrates the value of consistent adherence to objectives and strategy. All have clearly defined their users. All have targeted their service to these users in terms of scope and subject matter. All have maintained consistent quality of service. And all have delivered that service through distinctive treatment of subject matter: *The New York Times* in depth of coverage and the other four in distinctiveness of subject matter, presentation, and style. Each, within a constant purpose and framework of its own, provides the same general category of users with a flow of constantly new and appealing material.

These and other successful publications show the value of *consistent adherence to concepts,* which is the hallmark of every effective system of management. A publication makes regular, repeated impacts on its users. The cumulative impression of these impacts—favorable, neutral, or damaging—on the individual user determines whether he will buy or subscribe again. And the collective judgment of users determines whether circulation and advertising revenue, and share-of-market, will increase or decrease.

Most industrial companies have more in common with the brokerage business and with publications than is readily apparent. Every impression that any company makes on customers and prospective customers through its products, its advertising, and its people is favorable, neutral, or damaging. A clear set of strategic plans, geared to the established objectives of the business and enforced through its management system, will help make those impressions consistent. And if the plans are built around authentic and attractive user benefits, the impressions should be favorable and the company should prosper.

The strategies of Merrill Lynch and the publications I have mentioned are all available for their competitors to copy. The top managers of these businesses simply have applied a fact-founded approach, have carefully thought through what service their particular users want, and have developed and enforced strategic plans for delivering it. By so doing, they have consistently built favor with users through nearly every impression.

Their example can be useful to any business in developing and following its own system of management. In fact, it might be helpful to any management to think of its business as a publication being "edited" for "readers." Every day, customers and prospective customers are "reading" the business and deciding to "subscribe," to "renew," or to discontinue the "subscription." By thinking in these terms, managers are more likely to develop sound strategic plans and manage the business so as to make its impressions on the "readers" both attractive and consistent.

■ *Broadening and changing objectives.* The Wilkinson Sword Company has broadened and changed its objectives several times. When swords went out of fashion for fighting, it turned to other types of products using high-quality steel, such as quality garden tools and, most recently, the stainless steel razor blade. This strategy of repeatedly readapting a basic strength (in this case, metallurgical know-how) to new product lines often requires changes in the grand design of the company.

Such changes are difficult, but the difficulties can often be minimized by acquiring another company with the necessary know-how, facilities, and/or distribution. There are, of course, many other motives for mergers. They include smoothing out cyclical fluctuations in earnings, speeding up growth, improving per-share earnings, and increasing price of the common stock by improving the price/earnings ratio. The great urge to merge for these and other reasons has stimulated corporate-level strategic planning in the grand design of more and more companies every year.

For many years, under the brilliant direction of Paul L. Davies, until recently its long-time chief executive, the company now known as FMC Corporation has done outstanding strategic planning in changing its objectives and grand design. FMC had its origin in John Bean Manufacturing Company, which was itself a merger of two companies—one engaged in canning machinery manufacture and the other in manufacturing sprayers.

John Bean subsequently acquired a canning machinery company and two fresh fruit and vegetable packing house equipment companies. In 1929, the corporation changed its name to Food Machinery Company.

Paul Davies, who had been a banker before joining the company as treasurer, was dissatisfied with both the cyclical fluctuations of agricultural machinery earnings and the price/earnings ratio of the company's common stock. He decided that the rapidly growing chemical industry offered opportunities to smooth out the earnings fluctuations and improve the price/earnings ratio.

The first chemical acquisition, in 1943, was Niagara Sprayer & Chemical Company, an insecticide and pesticide business that served the eastern and southern states and provided a logical complement to the company's agricultural machinery business.

Niagara, in turn, absorbed two other agricultural chemical businesses that served agricultural territories in other parts of the United States and in one case made a different type of insecticide.

In 1948 FMC acquired Westvaco Chemical Company, a major company, followed by Ohio-Apex, Buffalo Electro-Chemical, the Fairfield plant of National Distillers, and others. Its chemical sales in 1948 were $20 million; its machinery sales, $58 million. By 1957, FMC chemical sales stood at $138 million and its machinery sales at $125 million, with $51 million more in defense sales.

Over that 10-year period, the objectives and grand design of the business had been fundamentally changed, earnings fluctuations had been minimized, and the price/earnings ratio significantly improved. These changes in objectives were reflected in two further name changes: in 1948 to Food Machinery and Chemical Corporation, and in 1961 to FMC Corporation.

In 1963, the company made another major acquisition, buying American Viscose Company's operating assets for $116 million in cash. This brought FMC into the manufacture and sale of rayon staple, tire and textile yarn, acetate yarn, and cellophane film. American Viscose's 1962 sales were nearly half of FMC's $506 million volume for that year.

By 1965, FMC annual sales of $928 million were well divided among chemicals, machinery, fibers, and films, reflecting growth from within in all product categories, as well as growth through acquisition. Profits for 1965 provided an after-tax return on investment of nearly 19 percent—ranking eleventh in return on investment among the hundred largest corporations.

FMC is an example of a truly remarkable strategic planning accomplishment. Paul Davies set objectives for the company to be achieved through acquisitions, and for many years he faithfully devoted a major part of his own time to the acquisition program. My observations indicate that any change in the grand design of a business requires the dedication of the chief executive and the devotion of a major part of his personal time to the task. That seems to be the only way to overcome the inertia and resistance to change that are inherent in carrying on the same old business.

■ *Coping with technological change.* Every business threatened by technological change (and all companies are) also has an opportunity to capitalize on it. If the technological change is substantial, significant revision in strategic plans will usually be necessary.

The National Commission on Technology, Automation, and Economic Progress appointed by President Johnson had this to say [9] about the rate of technological change:

> The pace of technological change has increased in recent decades and may increase in the future. . . . The process, however, is still a fairly long one. Our studies suggest that major technological discoveries may wait as long as 14 years before they reach commercial application even on a small scale, and perhaps another 5 years before their impact on the economy becomes large.

An increased rate of technological change of course calls for a speed-up in strategic planning. The Commission report is quite correct, however, in stating that the process of technological change is still a fairly long one. There is still ample time for any alert management to cope with problems created by technological change. The challenge is to capitalize on the *opportunities* it provides.

There are a number of basic reasons why technological change tends to be rather slow in business. They include concentration on meeting current orders, refining present practices, and increasing efficiency; failure to recognize problems or seize opportunity; the time required to work out technological problems of design and manufacture; difficulties of getting the new product to market; internal resistance to change; and user resistance to change. This user resistance is not caused merely by inertia and psychological resistance. The user may have real problems in adjusting to the use of the new product; if it is used as a component in his product, it may require technological change in other components, or in the end product itself. It is little wonder, therefore, that strategic planning to capitalize on technological change requires a command and leadership posture on the part of the chief executive.

An excellent example of varying rates of strategic responses to technological change is found in the classic case of the railroad locomotive industry. The eclipse of the steam engine by the diesel-electric came quite slowly. But through astute strategic planning, combined with poor strategic planning by its competitors, General Motors drove American Locomotive Company (Alco), the leader, out of business as an independent company and captured better than 75 percent of the business.

The diesel locomotive was used in Europe before it appeared in the United States. The first one was built by Swedish General Electric in 1913. In 1923, both General Electric (U.S.) and Alco built diesel-electric switching locomotives for yard work. The first road diesel was built by GM in 1934.

In 1935, Robert Binkerd, vice president of Baldwin Locomotive Works, told a meeting of the New York Railroad Club:

> Today we are having quite a ballyhoo about streamlined, lightweight trains and diesel locomotives, and it is no wonder the public feels that the steam locomotive is about to lay down and play dead. Yet over the years certain simple fundamental principles continue to operate. Some time in the

future, when all this is reviewed, we will not find our railroads any more dieselized than they are electrified.

In 1938, William Dickerman, chief executive of Alco, spoke to the Western Railway Club. He began, "Steam marches on," and he continued:

> For a century, as you know, steam has been the principal railroad motive power. It still is and, in my view, will continue to be. . . .
>
> True, other power units have challenged steam. This is as it should be. . . . But steam has graciously met every succeeding challenge to its supremacy and, I feel sure, will in due course meet and improve on this challenge, at less initial and operating cost, with no sacrifice of passenger safety and comfort. . . .
>
> The old iron horse literally breathes fire and water. It likes a challenge from youngsters like the electric and diesel-electric, especially in the spring of the year.
>
> It enjoys a race, is young for its years, simply will not be its age.

Yet these statements were made against a background of decline in industry production from roughly 2,000 locomotives in 1924 to 200 in 1931. And despite Alco's decline in net income from $8 million in 1926 to a $4 million *loss* in 1931, the company continued to pay dividends, thus weakening its financial position materially. The last steam locomotive was produced by Alco in 1963. By that time it had teamed up with General Electric to get that part of the diesel-electric business which GM had not captured. Baldwin had left the field entirely. In 1965, after some not very successful efforts to diversify, Alco became a division of Worthington Corporation.

Three major factors combined to bring about this dramatic shift in competitive position. First, steam locomotive managements failed to identify the threat of the diesel, which was visible as early as 1913. But GM—which also combined technological superiority with astute user strategies of service and financing—saw and seized the opportunity.

Second, the locomotive companies failed to develop the sophisticated research and development capability needed to perfect the diesel-electric.

Finally, when their competitive positions became critical, the locomotive companies lacked the financial resources for the job. (Before producing its first diesel, GM had spent an estimated $11 million.)

During the 1956 Senate Subcommittee investigation of General Motors, referred to earlier, Cyrus R. Osborn, head of GM's Electro-Motive Division, summarized this dramatic strategic planning example in these words:

> Customers' requirements and attitudes properly studied, evaluated, and acted upon at the proper time, have created our leading position in the diesel locomotive field; failure of our competitors to be competitive in this area has dictated their position in the industry.
>
> Mr. James M. Symes, president of the Pennsylvania Railroad, in a speech which he made in Chicago on September 7, 1955, stated: "The greatest single contribution to the economic and efficient operation of our railroads during my 40 years of association with the industry has been the development of the diesel locomotive. We all know the important part General Motors has played in that development. Today they have 23 million horsepower operating on our railroads in more than 16,000 diesel units, some of which have made between 2,500,000 and 3,500,000 miles and are still on the road performing quite satisfactorily. I would guess that this development alone is saving the railroads a minimum of $500 million a year—with initial investments being paid off in 3 to 4 years."
>
> Mr. Symes's feeling is shared by the entire railroad industry. It was earned honestly with a revolutionary new product and

a concept of standardization and service new in the railroad industry. It is precious to us and will be protected in the only way that such a reputation can be protected—namely, with continuing research, advanced engineering, and efficient manufacture always directed toward a superior product and superior service.

The report by the Senate Subcommittee staff summarized the situation this way:

> The Electro-Motive Division of General Motors Corporation presents a unique opportunity for the study of product innovation and entry into an established industry—locomotives. General Motors entered an industry which had utilized steam as its primary motive power for over a hundred years. Within 9 years after General Motors sold its first diesel locomotive, orders for locomotives powered by diesel engines exceeded steam locomotive orders, and, within 17 years, production of steam engines ceased entirely. The diesel locomotive revolutionized the railroad industry. General Motors can point to its entry into this field as an example of the operation of a progressive company at its best—entry into a new field, with a new product satisfying an economic need, and offering progressive reduction in the pricing of its product.

Fortunately for the economy, the rate of strategic response of the steam locomotive companies to technology is not typical. At the other end of the response-rapidity scale would probably be the airline, computer, and electronics industries. There have been several generations of airplanes and computers in rapid succession (although the DC-3 is still flying); and the response of the electronic industries generally to the transistor has been relatively rapid.

My observations of companies that do make rapid strategic responses show that the chief executive assumes a command and leadership position in strategic planning. For example, the dynamic strategic leadership provided by C. R. Smith for American Airlines and Thomas J. Watson, Jr., for IBM has enabled those companies, despite their great size, to capitalize swiftly on rapid technological change.

So if the rate of technological change is constantly quickening, strategic planning is becoming an increasingly important component of any management system. And the chief executive has an increasingly important personal leadership role to play in this basic element of managing.

The chief executive must make provision for keeping abreast of technological change and for evaluating the dangers and opportunities that each development presents to the business. He must decide on the timing of action. And when the time for action comes, he must use his command and leadership position to deal with the many sources of resistance to change inside and outside the business.

■ *Conflicting objectives: the fifty-fifty corporation.* During the course of a U.K. study, I asked a senior executive of a large British company to discuss his extensive experience with the fifty-fifty corporation—i.e., a corporation jointly owned by two companies. He retorted, "What is there to discuss? Just don't get mixed up in a fifty-fifty corporation. I'd rather have 49 percent ownership than 50 percent. With less than half the ownership, you can put pressure on the other fellow to do a good job of running the business. But with ownership divided, no one is in charge."

Having observed the internal management of a number of fifty-fifty corporations under a variety of conditions, and discussed their operations in confidence with many executives of fifty-fifty corporations, I believe they are inherently unsound. Since no two companies can hold to the same objectives very long, the jointly owned child gets caught between the two formerly compatible parents who later want to go their separate ways. The consequence is a family squabble with no good way of settling it.

Typically, executive loyalties within the fifty-fifty corporation are divided by the efforts of each parent company to develop its own camp of senior executives in the joint business. Sometimes the chief executive position of the fifty-fifty corporation is alternated between these two camps. Sometimes the incumbent belongs to neither camp and plays one off against the other. In any case, the problems resulting from conflicting objectives and divided loyalties often cause the jointly owned corporation to bog down in inaction. This usually results in gradual loss of the most talented executives, who dislike frustration and corporate politics and do not want to be associated with a business that is getting nowhere.

If the fifty-fifty corporation does prosper, as many have, it soon requires more capital. But by this time one parent or both may either lack the needed funds or have other, more attractive uses for them. Tension mounts between the two parents, and the child suffers.

Here are four examples of large, well-known, and generally successful fifty-fifty companies that required drastic action by their parents to cure them of corporate schizophrenia:

Ethyl Corporation. This company, jointly owned by GM and Standard Oil Company (New Jersey), was sold to Albemarle Paper Company.

Chemstrand Corporation. This nylon business was jointly owned by American Viscose and Monsanto until Monsanto bought the other half.

British Nylon Spinners. After a long and equally divided ownership by Imperial Chemical Industries and Courtaulds, ICI acquired all of the stock of this large U.K. enterprise.

Standard-Vacuum Corporation. Assets of this major international oil enterprise were divided between its two owners, Standard Oil Company (New Jersey) and Mobil Oil Company.

Many large fifty-fifty companies with less realistic parents are still struggling along under the stresses of joint ownership because the managements of the owning companies either will not face the facts or do not know the facts.

I do not maintain that the fifty-fifty corporation never provides a sound strategy. It has been widely used by American oil companies in raising the enormous amounts of capital needed to develop their international activities, and its effectiveness in these situations may well have fully justified the cost in terms of subsequent stresses in these joint ownerships. I do maintain, however, that before any company uses this grand design, it should squarely face the inherent limitations of the fifty-fifty corporation and realistically consider discontinuing it once its initial purpose has been served.

■ *External orientation of effective user strategy.* The foregoing examples of basic business strategy and company grand design show the importance of keeping user strategy oriented to the environment of the business. This means constantly gathering and evaluating the facts on the external forces at work. Hazardous forces must be countered, and favorable forces should be turned to advantage.

In planning user strategy, therefore, top managers—especially marketing managers—should keep looking outside the business. Excessive top-management preoccupation with matters inside the business can result in serious loss of competitive position. In the most successful companies, top management is sensitive and alert to the future and to the outside forces that affect, or might affect, the businesses in which the company is or might be engaged.

Profit Strategy

When user strategy has been determined, the chief executive and his cabinet can turn to profit strategy. Knowing the general level of profit to which their user strategy entitles them, they can develop their profit strategy accordingly. In comparison with user strategy, the development of profit strategy requires more top-management attention to internal factors. Even so, the effects of external forces on each profit factor must also be carefully evaluated.

But it is one thing to be entitled to a profit and quite another to convert potential profit into dollars. That conversion brings into focus the importance of effective administration—which should begin with the development of a specific profit strategy based on user strategy.

Every successful company has some form of profit strategy. All I want to do here is suggest an approach to profit strategy, distilled from the experiences of many large and successful corporations.

■ *Profit-factor analysis.* The first step is to analyze the relative importance of each factor or element affecting profits. The object is to determine specifically and factually how profits are earned, by analyzing each factor of income, cost, and expense and assessing the relative profit impact of each. A break-even chart for each business is a useful device because it shows visually the impact of volume, price, and product mix on profits.

In perfume, for example, ingredients are a relatively low cost factor, while in cement they are high. Some products have a high labor cost; in others, labor is a relatively low cost factor. For some companies, profit is heavily influenced by sources of raw material; for example, the most profitable petroleum companies acquire a high proportion of their own sources of crude oil and buy the balance in the open market. Profits of telephone, gas, and electric companies depend heavily on ability to raise large amounts of new capital to provide expensive facilities.

Thus, the best profit strategy is based on a deep under-standing of the profit economics of the business—the economics of income, cost, and expense, and the real influence of each factor on ultimate profits. I find that the top management ex-ecutives of the most successful companies have such an under-standing and keep the key profit factors in the forefront of their thinking.

Air Express International Corporation, an international air freight forwarding business, provides a good example of profit strategy. The user strategy of AEI is based on providing shippers with a comprehensive and convenient service. It moves air freight in any quantity on one airbill, to and from any points in the world, expediting customs clearances and doing the whole job door to door. AEI provides the airlines with a way to sell "perishable" excess cargo space. It does all the paper work, ac-counting, and collection for the airlines and provides them with other services as well.

AEI's profit strategy, as distinguished from its user strategy, is based on four primary factors: (1) getting the air-cargo space or "raw material" at favorable rates, (2) selling the space at satisfactory margins, (3) developing and staffing offices around the world to provide the services, and (4) managing the whole system efficiently. Once the basic structure of offices has been built and is operating efficiently, added volume provides profit leverage. But in this business, attention to these key profit fac-tors is not enough; success also requires much attention to overall efficiency—that is, to effectiveness, productivity, and low cost. And here the company has thus far been deficient.

Over-all efficiency in that sense can, of course, contribute to the profits of *every* company, so it should be part of every profit strategy. But its relative importance varies from business to business.

To sum up, the end product of the profit-factor analysis is a precise determination of the critical factors affecting profit, and their relative importance, as well as of the relative importance of overall efficiency.

■ *Rank-ordering management emphasis.* The profit-factor analysis provides the basis for management determination of the order of importance of each factor in earning maximum profits. The will to manage can then be applied most resolutely to the most critical of the key factors. For example, activities involving these factors can be nourished with more capital and higher-caliber executive manpower.

The following examples show how leading companies have supplemented sound user strategies with emphasis on key profit factors.

■ Du Pont stresses research and development. Its financial commitment to R & D is large, both relatively and absolutely. Manpower commitment, both in numbers and excellence, is substantial. Special incentives have been developed to improve performance, and performance-evaluation procedures have been "manicured." Steps to convert research results into salable products are under constant study.

Du Pont makes no secret of its deep dedication to research and development. The company's constant stream of new products is the clear consequence of a strategic decision to devote sizable amounts of time, money, manpower, and management attention to research and development on a carefully administered basis.

■ Procter & Gamble makes advertising a feature of both its user and profit strategies. The company stands consistently at or near the top of the lists of advertisers ranked by size of annual expenditures. Perhaps equally important are the time, thought, and attention that top management gives to advertising. The more advanced concepts and procedures that have resulted make P & G's relatively large expenditures relatively more productive as well.

■ IBM supports its user strategy of superior customer service with massive devotion to training. The company not only trains its own personnel in how to sell, install, and service its machines, but also trains customer personnel in how to use them. IBM's competitive advantage of superior customer service has come about in the same old way: careful and consistent application of thought, money, manpower, time, and management attention to a strategically important profit factor.

■ Two leading companies made drastic changes in their methods of distribution to customers because increasing costs of distribution were cutting into profits. One company gave up door-to-door selling and successfully shifted to established retail channels, with a resulting increase in volume and substantial decrease in selling cost. Another company gave up its own direct selling and warehouse system with the same results.

Thus the economics of the industry—and changes in the economics—should control the strategies of the companies in it. In the oil industry, for example, changes from time to time in the relative profit importance of controlling crude oil reserves and marketing outlets caused major changes in company strategy; and the profitability of various companies was largely determined by their respective configurations, resulting from the different forms of integration they adopted. Similar integration phenomena occurred in aluminum companies and forest product industries; as the economics of these industries changed, the companies whose managements understood the changes and adjusted their strategies accordingly were the ones that profited most.

These examples point up a simple but powerful lesson: The managements of the most successful companies gain a deep understanding of the factors controlling the profits of their companies and of the separate businesses that make them up. Then they see to it that the key activities get proper priorities in money, manpower, and top-management attention. Given these priorities, managers at all levels can move purposefully to develop high productivity at optimum cost in the activities that really count.

In contrast, the managements of less successful companies tend to have a more superficial understanding of what really makes their companies profitable. Consequently, their strategic decisions on where to put money, manpower, and management attention are less soundly based; and managers at all levels move less purposefully, with resulting lower productivity and higher costs. Because the will to manage the critical profit activities is less resolute in these companies, their profit results are naturally less satisfactory.

Executive Manpower Strategy

People in IBM recall a story told of Thomas J. Watson, Sr., founder of the company. During the worst of the depression of the thirties, he met a friend who expressed surprise that IBM was still hiring salesmen. Mr. Watson replied, "Some men, as they grow older, turn to drinking and women. *I* collect salesmen." As part of its strategy, IBM has consistently hired high-caliber, college-trained salesmen in substantial numbers—and it continues to do so. This has given the company great strength in serving its customers—and many of these men have moved up to the highest levels of management.

Since business faces a worldwide shortage of high-talent manpower, executive manpower administration has become vital to every company. For this reason, I will take it up in detail in Chapter 6. Here I simply want to emphasize the importance to every company of taking a *strategic* approach to executive manpower development—that is, shaping its user and profit strategies to the executive manpower needs of the business.

It is not enough to recite clichés about the importance of capable executives to business success. If they *are* important, then the basic strategy of the business—and the way it is managed—should be shaped accordingly. For example, a business that depends heavily on research and development must not only attract scientifically trained personnel but also create a working atmosphere that will help retain them and make them productive.

As part of its profit-factor analysis, management should assess the importance of manpower to any critical activity— especially the number and caliber of supervisors and managers required now and in the future. For unless the company is administered so as to attract and motivate the required complement of personnel, neither its user strategy nor its profit strategy can be fully effective.

Although executive manpower has always been regarded as critical to business success, I find that only a few of the best-managed companies really think of it in strategic terms. Currently, for example, progressive top-management executives in retailing and commercial banking are concerned about the inability of their industries to attract a fair share of talent from leading graduate business schools. Yet few retailers or banks have taken a strategic approach to their management manpower problems.

Henning Prentis, long the chief executive of Armstrong Cork Company, once told me that a major reason for diversifying the company by acquiring "run-down" businesses was to give all the young management trainees he was bringing into the company "something to chew on and more places to go." Here was a broadening of corporate objectives made as part of the company's manpower strategy. It paid off by providing Armstrong with real depth of management talent.

To repeat: user strategy, profit strategy, and executive manpower strategy are closely interrelated, but better results will be attained by first approaching each separately and then adjusting each to support the others. Considering the shortage of high-talent business manpower that is likely to prevail during the next decade, a carefully developed executive manpower strategy can provide most companies with an important competitive advantage; and user and profit strategies should be adjusted accordingly.

Strategic Leadership

In a conversation I had some years ago with Clifford Backstrand, who followed Henning Prentis as chief executive of Armstrong Cork, he mentioned one broadly applicable factor that contributed to his company's competitive dominance in the hard-surface floor covering field. Here, in substance, is what he told me:

> We try to move ahead on our own—not copy others. Our competitors can learn *what* we do, so they can copy us. But they can't tell *why* we do it, so they can't do it as well. The things of ours that they copy won't fit well into their total plans. And, by the time they copy us, we'll have developed something new. Competitive copiers are always off stride.

That certainly applies to all phases of strategy—user, profit, and executive manpower. The company that leads in setting objectives and developing strategy is likely to keep its competitive copiers off stride. Instead of being able to develop a carefully planned total effort, copiers must improvise; and improvisation is usually less effective and nearly always more costly.

The strategic leader also has a time advantage. It will take competitors a long time to overcome the high-talent manpower lead that IBM and Armstrong Cork have established. Indeed, if these companies adhere effectively to the same strategy, about all their competitors will be able to do is to match this important competitive strength.

Moreover, strategic plans are difficult to copy because they are the product of fact-finding, analysis, and creative thinking. As Mr. Blancke of Celanese said, "Planning is the intellectual arm of organized growth"—and intellectual activity is difficult to copy. It is well known that Du Pont is extra strong in the laboratory and that IBM is extra strong in the market place. But their competitors do not match the dedication of Du Pont's or IBM's management to these strategic factors—nor do they know the scores of ways in which each company maintains its particular competitive advantage. And even if they did, the competitors would find it difficult and time consuming to modify their systems and structures of priorities in order to accommodate to these changes.

In short, the management that thinks in strategic terms and can be first with effective strategic plans possesses a powerful competitive weapon. It is also, in a sense, a secret weapon: only the physical manifestations of objectives and strategy are accessible to competitors. The leaders are in command; they can plan deliberately and execute thoroughly. Those who copy must scramble to catch up when the *results* of the leader's strategy become known; and the scrambler, off stride, cannot make and execute plans as thoroughly or effectively.

Rudyard Kipling put it this way:

> They copied all they could follow
> But they couldn't copy my mind,
> And I left 'em sweating and stealing
> A year-and-a-half behind.[10]

Lessons from the Leaders

From comparing, behind the scenes, the user, profit, and manpower strategies of many leading companies with those of the rest of the pack, I have gained these convictions:

- The top-management executives of the leaders have a deeper understanding of their strategic facts. They have a more specific knowledge of what users need and want. They are more sharply aware of forces at work in the company environment, as determined by specific depth analysis of industry outlook and the competitive strengths and weaknesses of each product group in each major market. These executives set priorities on the basis of more searching profit-factor analysis. And they have more facts about executive manpower needs, capabilities, and attitudes. In short, they dig for facts—and then use them.

- Top-management executives of the leaders look at the strategic facts more objectively. They are willing to recognize and face problems. They are alert to opportunities. And they are willing to provide leadership to effect the internal changes in strategy required to cope with problems and seize opportunities. They have a sense of urgency.

- In setting objectives and developing strategies, the top-management executives of the most successful companies are determined to lead rather than to follow.

■ The top-management executives of the leaders believe in their strategies and follow them. They devote money, manpower, and especially their own time to the activities of primary strategic importance. Their attention to these activities is more resolute and consistent—they act with purposeful devotion.

■ Yet the margins of resource superiority of leading companies over their nearest competitors are often not very great—nor do they need to be. Essentially, their superior strategic plans, as well as their margins of over-all success, flow from a more resolute will to manage, applied more consistently by top-management executives.

■ Finally, the top-management executives of the leaders learn to *think and act in strategic terms*. That is, they learn to recognize and relate the significance of individual developments to the over-all long-term health, growth, and profits of the company.

4

Policies, Standards, and Procedures: Guidelines for Gearing Action to Strategy

I once asked my wife why she does most of her supermarket buying at the A & P. She replied without hesitation, "They take back their merchandise without making you feel guilty about it. Other stores usually take things back, too, but they're so grudging about it that you wish you'd never brought the whole thing up."

"Is it A & P, or is it the manager?" I asked.

"It must be A & P," she said, "because they've had several managers at our store since I started trading there."

The next time we went to the A & P, I noticed a large sign, nicely framed and under glass, on the wall near the check-out counters. In letters nearly three inches high, it read:

THE A & P POLICY

Always to:
> Do what is honest, fair, sincere and in the best interest of every customer
> Extend friendly, satisfying service to everyone
> Give every customer the most good food for her money
> Assure accurate weight every time—16 ounces to each pound

Give accurate count and full measure

Charge the correct price

Cheerfully refund customers' money if for any reason any
purchase is not satisfactory

The Great Atlantic and Pacific Tea Company

The same statement of customer policy is clearly displayed,
as a guide to employees and as a sales appeal to customers, on
the walls of some 4,500 A & P stores throughout the country.
The sign also provides subtle employee discipline. Knowing
that customers will read A & P's promise and expect it to be
kept, employees in all 4,500 A & P stores have an added reason
to follow the policy faithfully.

How much its customer policy alone has helped increase
A & P's share-of-market would be hard to say. But through its
strategy and policies, A & P has become the world's largest food
chain, with fiscal 1964 sales of $5.1 billion, over $2 billion
more than its nearest competitor, Safeway.

The Nature of Policy

Basically, a policy is *a plan for action in prescribed circumstances*. Its function is well described in the foreword to the
50th anniversary edition (1950) of a booklet of basic company
policies published by Armco Steel Corporation:

> To chart a course for all to follow in the conduct of com-
> pany business, sound management establishes certain policies,
> developed by experience and tested by time, that all who play
> a part, no matter what its importance, may understand the
> official position of the institution. *Policies are, in short, the
> organization's constitution of intention, decision, and action.*
> [Italics supplied.]

Here is one of the policies stated in the booklet: "To be
consistent and *persistent* in the application of Armco Policies

to each and every situation." In another sense, then, policy is *a guide to action in carrying out the strategic plans of the business.* Properly geared to strategy, it is the most pervasive action-guiding component of the programmed management system.

In A & P's case, the returned-goods policy tells thousands of clerks throughout the country to give the customer her money back willingly and pleasantly, whenever she asks for it—a simple but powerful guide to *action* with an enormous total impact when carried out in all 4,500 stores. Note, too, that this policy (like other A & P policies) is closely geared to A & P's strategy of doing a volume business at low prices. Since the purpose of a policy is to guide the actions of people, policies that are geared to strategy and consistently followed help to make strategic plans effective.

Further insight into the nature and use of policies is provided by George S. Dively, chief executive of Harris-Intertype Corporation:

> The modern trend in effective corporate management, as I see it, is to provide more clearly defined guide policies at the top, delegate a great deal of authority and responsibility to carefully developed profit centers at the operating level, and then implement a rather wide range of vehicles for "up and down" communication, consultation, advice, and guidance in the area between, where policy making and administration are integrated or merged.
>
> Where applicable, the concept of centralized policy making and decentralized administration seems to provide a most effective organization structure for achieving these objectives. Although these broad management principles have been applied for years by some of our country's largest and best-known corporations, the approach is continually being refined, and, as the development of professional management skills in-

creases, it is becoming applicable to more and more smaller and medium-size companies.[1]

Indeed, policies carefully geared to strategy do facilitate delegation and do help make strategy effective in action, especially when people have been trained to believe in and carry out a systems approach to administration. And policies are as important a managing process in government or a labor organization as they are in business. For example, President Johnson's 1965 Defense Message to Congress defined ten "basic policies" that guide the defense establishment. And John L. Lewis, in his letter of resignation as president of the United Mine Workers (December 15, 1959), charged its members to "keep your union strong, its policies sound, and give loyal support to the officers and representatives who serve you."

Since policy is a plan for action *in prescribed circumstances,* by specifying the circumstances in which a particular policy becomes operative, top management determines in advance what people shall do when such circumstances occur. The quantity discount provides a simple example: beyond a prescribed quantity point, company people charge the customers a lower price.

Let's consider a more complex example of the prescribed-circumstance aspect of policy making. An automobile company division found that many customers were having trouble with the transmission of a particular model. After investigation, management decided that it would be better to replace than repair the transmission. A policy bulletin to that effect was sent out to all dealers, covering that particular year and model and spelling out just how the whole problem should be dealt with and how the division would reimburse the dealer.

In making policy, a manager can carefully think through in advance specifically how people should perform under particular, prescribable circumstances. The probable cost and other consequences of the policy—as well as the consequences of not establishing a policy—can and should be taken into account.

A good example is seen in a folder, "Our Basic Policies," in which the largest brokerage firm, Merrill Lynch, Pierce, Fenner & Smith, prescribes how its thousands of employees in more than 160 offices throughout the world shall act in particular circumstances. Like the customer policy posted in A & P's food stores, that folder also tells customers what to expect of Merrill Lynch account executives in particular circumstances. So again a clear statement of policies with customer appeal becomes a builder of customer goodwill and a valuable corporate image, as well as a working part of the programmed management system.

Full understanding of the nature and power of policy requires appreciation of the consequences and costs of having no stated policy. Consider chain stores that have no clear-cut returned-goods policy comparable to A & P's. In those chains each manager must make the policy for his store. The clerk refers each case to the manager, who decides it according to his own judgment—and may later have to justify the decision to his superior. If there are differences of opinion, the communications required to settle them will incur time and other costs. The internal costs of dealing with numerous transactions without clear guidelines, augmented by the loss of customer goodwill, can mount into substantial figures. In addition, the confusion and frustration resulting from the absence of a clearly stated policy are likely to reduce both morale and productivity.

Lack of clear-cut policy also weakens top-management control. After a reasonable period of catch-as-catch-can decision making on any issue, subordinates tend to act on the assumption that their superiors will make substantially the same decisions under similar circumstances. Thus, a policy evolves out of practice.

That process would work pretty well in the absence of management turnover. But with any change of people in the line of command, the old unwritten policy may be superseded by changed practice. Unless the new manager finds out about the practices of his predecessor and adopts them himself, the process of trial and error must start all over again. And it must continue until the new manager's practice, based on his own personal judgments, becomes established as policy with his subordinates.

If any top executive of a large-scale enterprise wants a subject for nightmares, he can dream of the cost and other consequences of hundreds or even thousands of people engaged in hundreds of different activities, with their practices crystallizing into policies over which he has little or no effective control. He can avoid such nightmares by providing well-thought-out and clearly stated policies on every important type of activity. Then everyone down the line can act with confidence, dispatch, and optimum cost.

No business, of course, can or should establish policies covering every type of action. That would make for cumbersome administration and prove stultifying to the people in the organization, who want room to exercise their own discretion, judgment, and common sense. Here company philosophy comes into play: "The way we do things around here" in effect provides policy guidance for a wide range of actions and decisions for which it would not be sensible to have written policies.

In most companies, however, the simplicity and power of

policy making are inadequately recognized; and in nearly every company, this managing process can be much more fully exploited in achieving success.

Interrelationship between Strategy and Policy

Sometimes a brilliant new policy can revolutionize a business. It did Procter & Gamble. Colonel Procter, an outstanding pioneer in personnel relations, believed that steady employment was socially desirable. In 1923, therefore, P & G established a policy of providing 48 standard workweeks of employment in each calendar year to every worker who had been with the company two years, who worked effectively, and who would take any job he was given.

Then and now, that is advanced personnel relations policy —and in order to carry it out the P & G business had to be virtually made over. In a remarkable speech in 1945, Richard R. Deupree, then and for many years chief executive of the company, described how the steady-employment policy, designed to be socially desirable, was made highly profitable as well.[2] Here are some of the changes and their effects, as described by Mr. Deupree:

- The sales department arranged for regular customer shipments by using 30- to 45-day forward shipments and providing price protection. Customers were never out of stock, and the new policy benefited both company and distributors.

- To take care of periods when dealers could not accept forward orders, the company arranged storage facilities (owned and leased) for a minimum of one month's supply and a maximum of two. As a result, inventories were better balanced and kept at lower levels.

- The generally even level of manufacture permitted substantial reductions in manufacturing costs. Regular buying permitted the company to get lower prices from suppliers. Plant investment was substantially lower, because capacity to take care of peak periods was no longer needed. Between 1923 and 1945, Mr. Deupree estimated, the plant investment saving was $100 million.

■ Labor relations problems were minimized and worker morale and productivity improved, producing probably the greatest benefits of all.

Although the steady-employment policy was not simple to put into effect, it is and was, in Mr. Deupree's words, "probably the greatest thing in our company." Thus a farsighted and courageous personnel policy was the genesis of new policies in marketing, manufacturing, and general management that reached out to influence the user, profit, and manpower strategies of the company. In fact, the P & G steady-employment policy is so fundamental that it is almost a company goal. Altogether, the case of P & G clearly illustrates the interactions and interdependencies between policy and strategy, which are characteristic of management programs in successful companies.

Sometimes policy actually becomes identical with strategy. *The New York Times* is a case in point. When Adolph S. Ochs assumed control of *The Times* in 1896, he published a declaration of principles containing these words:

> It will be my earnest aim that *The New York Times* give the news, all the news, in concise and attractive form . . . and give it as early, if not earlier, than it can be learned through any other reliable medium; to give the news impartially, without fear or favor, regardless of any party, sect or interest involved; to make the columns of *The New York Times* a forum for the consideration of all questions of public

importance, and to that end to invite intelligent discussion from all shades of opinion.

Some years ago, writing in *The New York Times Magazine,* Robert McLean, publisher of *The Philadelphia Bulletin* and former president of the Associated Press, commented on this creed—which was a statement of policy, objective, and strategy. Adolph Ochs, Mr. McLean wrote:

> . . . was to follow [it] scrupulously from the day he acquired *The Times* until his death thirty-nine years later on April 8, 1935. The creed was simplicity itself—yet at the time it appears to have been observed more in the breach than in the fact. Its application year in and out to the daily business of newspaper making made a striking and lasting contribution to journalism in New York City, in the nation and to an extent throughout the world.[3]

Mr. McLean tells how Ochs's "unfaltering drive to give the news impartially . . . touched intimately every department of the organization and every person associated with the enterprise." Ochs's example, he observes, "demonstrated that in the most highly competitive market true values are the enduring ones . . . and that only those newspapers and institutions that serve the people well will have their continued support." As Mr. McLean's article shows, *The Times's* continuing competitive strength rests firmly on consistent adherence to a long-established policy so fundamental that it amounts to a basic strategy.

By using the system approach, any management can capitalize on the close relationships among policy, strategy, and the other managing processes. The integration of managing processes resulting from the system approach reinforces the will to manage; gives the whole enterprise greater user impact that increases volume and share-of-market; and helps reduce costs, increase organizational effectiveness, and stimulate the development of future managers.

The Power of Policy

As *The New York Times* story shows, great competitive power flows from simple policies, flexibly adapted to different and changing conditions but consistently adhered to.

The movement of American business overseas provides an excellent laboratory for analysis of policy under different conditions. Back in 1956 Stanley C. Allyn, then president of National Cash Register Company, was asked to tell a Harvard Business School alumni conference why his company had been so successful overseas. (At that time its overseas volume was more than $100 million, or about 40 percent of sales.) Mr. Allyn outlined nine principles that he termed "fundamentals of our working pattern." [4] They included the following policies:

> ■ We try to give the foreign market the product which the market wants—and not the product which we think the market ought to have.
> ■ We believe in staffing our overseas operations with natives of the countries. [At that time just six of NCR's 18,000 overseas employees were Americans.]
> ■ We do not treat our overseas employees as stepchildren.
> ■ We are extremely careful to respect the customs, traditions, religions and sensitivities of alien peoples.

Undeniably, these policies are simple, even obvious. Yet I could name a number of outstanding American companies that either ignore the obvious in their overseas operations or, while professing similar policies, do a miserable job of following them.

Let's consider overseas product policy. One machinery manufacturer, which is dominant in the U.S. market, sells the identical products overseas. The managements of its overseas subsidiaries have pleaded for permission to adapt the operating characteristics and specifications of these machines to customer requirements, and also permit them to be priced more competitively. The wisdom of this course seems obvious. But, unlike NCR, the U.S. parent company management has turned down every such proposal on grounds that it is not interested in manufacturing "low quality" machines. Today the strong overseas market position which this company established before its basic patents had expired is being rapidly eroded.

Such lack of flexibility in adapting product policy to new conditions is a surprisingly common error among American companies with capable managements that are unsophisticated in overseas operations. What is even more surprising is to find even British managements, which generally *are* sophisticated in overseas operations, making the same error when entering the U.S. market.

As companies move overseas, simple and successful policies are too frequently "left at home"—truly a costly oversight when the established policy could be profitably applied to overseas operations. The executive who is not capable enough to be promoted in the United States—sometimes even the executive who has failed in a domestic assignment—is too often sent overseas, where a strange language and unfamiliar conditions and customs typically compound the difficulties of managing. In some cases overseas posts are even filled with untrustworthy expatriate and foreign personnel, in sharp violation of policies and standards proven successful at home. Yet the unhappy consequences of such overseas assignments often seem to come as both a surprise and a disappointment to the U.S. management.

Here again, the fact-founded approach should be applied: Get the *overseas* facts. Establish the policies and offer the products that conditions *there* dictate. Don't assume that overseas conditions and attitudes are the same as in the United States; probably both will be different.

But it is not only overseas that simple, powerful policies are disregarded. Here at home, for example, the policy of field-testing all new products before putting them on the market may collapse under the pressures of time and competition. I recall urging the president of a leading air-conditioning manufacturer not to put a new window air conditioner on the market without the field test that the company's policy prescribed. The advice was obvious—but the president decided to leave out the field test just the same. The new product, he argued, was made up of "well-tested components," and running a field test would mean missing a whole sales season. As it turned out, every one of the first 2,500 deliveries had to be returned, and the season was missed anyway. From that time on, there were no more exceptions to the policy of field-testing new products!

Resolute adherence to policy is a hallmark of the will to manage found in successful companies. Adherence to soundly conceived policies develops sinews of consistency that help to increase corporate effectiveness, reduce costs, and build a clear corporate image. Thus if A & P's employees follow the policies posted on the walls of all stores, effectiveness will be greater, costs lower, and market impact enormous. Adherence to policy is an essential aspect of Benjamin Disraeli's success pattern, "constancy to purpose."

But consistency should not imply rigidity. Adherence to policy provides power only when the policy is sound—and it cannot be sound unless it is adapted to differing conditions. Liebmann Breweries, Inc., found that policies that helped make its Rheingold beer the biggest seller in New York City did not work well in Los Angeles. In New York, Liebmann distributes direct to stores and bars through its own fleet of 1,000 trucks. But in Los Angeles, with its vast geographical spread and the local practice of using distributors, the company's direct distribution policy was ineffective. Likewise, Liebmann's gigantic annual "Miss Rheingold" contest, so successful in New York, was a flop in Los Angeles. Speculating on its failure to impress anybody, *Business Week* observed at the time: "One reason may be that Los Angeles is up to its ears in beauty queens, mecca of the aspiring motion picture star." [5]

In short, as Phillip Liebmann, the company's president, frankly put it, "We tried to fit patterns that suited New York to the Los Angeles market."

Steps in Making Policy

Since policy making provides top management with a powerful means for making its will to manage effective throughout the business, top managers of the most successful companies devote substantial time to strengthening this managing process. They know the importance of making conscious, factually based choices among carefully developed alternatives. If no such choice is made, then (since people must act) an existing policy will be followed, or—through trial and error from hastily considered individual decisions—some practice will be evolved that, in effect, becomes policy.

Gaining the full power of policy is a challenge to any management—a challenge that no simple formula can adequately meet. Here is an approach distilled from the experience of successful companies:

1. A policy should be simple, geared to factually deter-

mined realities (i.e., forces at work outside and inside the business), rooted in common sense, and anchored to enduring values. Policies that meet these tests will also be more readily accepted, believed in, and adhered to by company people. And customers must accept and believe in some policies if the company is to build a favorable corporate image at reasonable cost.

2. In developing a policy, facts should be gathered about the conditions under which the policy will operate, especially the external conditions. Policies should not be based too largely on "experience," because this is usually culled from people's memories of past circumstances and events—memories that are often colored by personal interpretations of what actually happened, why it happened, and what it means as a guide for future action. Personal judgments are, of course, essential ingredients in establishing any policy. But during the analysis that precedes final formulation of the policy, fact and opinion should be separated as sharply as possible.

3. The best policy results from consideration of all feasible action alternatives, not just the first few possibilities that come to mind. The manager responsible should require the development of a number of alternate plans of action. These should be developed clearly and specifically, and facts—including probable results and costs—gathered about each. Writing about government policy making, Robert R. Bowie, director of policy planning in the State Department, says it like this:

> . . . The policy-maker works in the uneasy world of prediction and probability. On the basis of the available intelligence, his job is (1) to determine what alternative courses of action are feasible and (2) to choose which to pursue.
>
> The possible alternatives are not self-evident. Identifying and formulating them requires both analysis and imagination.

And in choosing among them, one must guard against disaster, should the unexpected occur, while avoiding that cautious hedging which forfeits the advantages of any single course by straddling several.[6]

That is good advice for the policy maker in business: reach for all possible alternatives.

4. In business as in government policy, the policy maker's task is to choose the alternative which, in the light of all the facts and probabilities, offers the optimum balance between cost and effectiveness. In other words, he *makes* policy by choosing the course or plan of action to be followed regularly in the prescribed circumstances.

In deciding complex policy questions—with many alternatives to choose from and many facts affecting each—a computer may help make the optimum choice, or at least facilitate consideration of a broad range of choices. For example, a computer can be extremely helpful in determining machine and plant utilization alternatives as markets shift and transportation costs change.

5. Whenever basic conditions change, established policies should be reexamined. Time, technology, and geography create new conditions. Competition may need to be countered or company leadership reestablished. Political and social developments may set new forces in motion. Shifts in population makeup may create new problems to cope with or provide new opportunities to seize.

Rigidity of policy in the face of different and changed conditions can be disastrous. But the simpler the policy and the more firmly anchored in enduring values, the less frequent will be the need for change—permitting greater consistency of action, which, of course, results in lower cost and greater effectiveness.

6. Until there *is* a need for change, *the policy should be*

followed. Too many exceptions will destroy a policy. Weak enforcement of policy increases costs, reduces effectiveness, and causes loss of respect for management. A resolute will to manage is reflected in resolute adherence to policy.

Standards

Like a policy, a standard in managing—meaning, of course, a measure, criterion, norm, or test of performance or action—provides a guideline for gearing action to strategy. A standard can make a policy more effective by giving it precision. Reinforced by explicit standards, a policy becomes easier and quicker to carry out, because people know *how* to follow it.

As we will see in a later chapter, standards (or criteria) for selecting people are factors of great importance to company success. Ethical standards apart, this does not mean that a *high* standard is necessarily the soundest or the most profitable standard. For example, although high-caliber people will generally produce high profits, successful companies have found it unwise to put people into positions where their training or intellectual capacity will go to waste. The optimum standard is one that strikes the balance between cost and performance (or results) which produces the maximum *long-term* net profit.

Surprisingly often, this simple, even obvious concept is violated or ignored by otherwise capable managers. Take the case of plant construction standards. The profits of one large divisionalized business I know will be sapped for years by the unnecessarily high standards used in constructing many of its plants over a stretch of fifteen years. During this period, the manufacturing vice president had charge of constructing plants for all divisions. His department determined the type of construction to be used; the division manager could not effectively question it.

Since the vice president demanded high standards, all the

new plants were over-engineered, with resulting over-investment of capital or high operating costs or both. These "gold-plated" plants, through which the vice president (now retired) was fond of conducting visitors, are still showcases. But the division executives who are responsible for using them in profitable production call them "monuments."

Let me emphasize parenthetically: Under a programmed management system, that vice president could not have imposed his construction standards on the divisions without challenge. As will be seen later, programmed management would have permitted any division manager to have challenged any standard established by that (or any other) functional executive; and if necessary, the chief executive would have made the final decision.

As another example of optimizing, let's take standards for purchasing policies. Although price is too frequently the dominant standard here, optimization of performance and price is common in progressive purchasing departments. In fact, the most advanced purchasing in effect coordinates the business of the buying company with that of the supplier, fitting the needs of the one to the capabilities of the other for the benefit of both. Sears, Roebuck pioneered this approach by buying from major suppliers in their off-season, but Sears and other companies have carried the approach much further than that.

Operating performance standards, of course, have important effects on costs and customer relations. For example, many companies that specify a maximum time period between receipt and shipment of orders find that reduction of a day or two in the "lateness" standard can provide a useful competitive service edge. And customer service standards are often an important part of a company's competitive strategy.

The steps in setting a standard (i.e., a performance test or criterion) for any activity are similar to those involved in making policy: Select a variety of possible alternative standards; study the probable costs and results of each; select the alternative that presents the optimum balance of costs and results. The resulting standard will become another guideline for action.

Procedures

Procedures, or specified steps to be taken in carrying out a policy in accordance with established standards, are a third guideline for gearing action to strategy. Procedures are of course less important than either policy or standard guidelines, but they deserve more attention than they ordinarily get. For, by specifying how the action is to be carried out, the procedure influences its cost. And it may determine whether a standard is met at all.

For example, a company may establish a policy of "prompt delivery" for all shipments and set 48 hours after receipt of the order as the standard of promptness for a particular line of products. Whether this standard is met will depend importantly on the procedures established for transmitting orders to the right plant or warehouse and for filling and shipping the order. And certainly those procedures will influence the cost of order-handling.

The value of procedure analysis has long been recognized in plants and offices, where great attention has been paid to work simplification and work flow. But major opportunities for improving procedures still exist in most businesses. This is especially true where major procedures operate across departmental lines, because in such cases only the chief executive of the division or the company is responsible for all the activities involved.

Writing Up the Guidelines

Policies, standards, and procedures are obviously of little use as guidelines for action unless they are followed. Just as obviously, they can't be followed unless they are known to the people whose actions they are supposed to guide. Yet disdain for written policies is perplexingly prevalent in business. There is indifference, even resistance, to the idea of putting policies, standards, and procedures into writing.

The best-managed companies, of course, do just that. Not only do they publish their policies in bulletin form, but in many cases they bind them in looseleaf manuals or "guides" (a more appealing term) for ready reference.

One reason for written guidelines, of course, is that they are easily transmitted to all concerned. Word-of-mouth is a slow and often inaccurate means of communicating what should be blueprints for action. Labor legislation and collective bargaining with unions have greatly stimulated management to commit personnel policies to writing, and most companies now put their basic personnel policies into pamphlets for employees. The same logic applies to major policies in other areas.

But there are at least two more advantages to written policies, standards, and procedures. First, putting anything in writing enforces more thorough and precise thinking. In starting a series of general policy statements, one able chief executive issued this statement: "These policy bulletins were started some months ago as a means of gradually hammering out and reducing to writing those policy matters that require coordination between the General Office Staff and the operating organizations."

In discussing "corporate policy bulletins," George Dively of Harris-Intertype Corporation said in the speech mentioned earlier: "The underlying corporate philosophy and the reasoning behind it are set forth in each bulletin, so that division managers can understand the 'why' of the policy concerned."

Second, by circulating written drafts to those who should participate in formulating the policy and to some of those who will be affected by it, more facts, more imagination, more alternatives, and more points of view can be brought to bear on the finished job. By participating in this review process, those who will be affected can also help to clarify the meaning of the final statement.

I recall a conversation on a company plane that brought both these points home vividly. My host was the new chief executive of a company with sales just under a billion dollars. His other guest on this flight was the experienced chief executive of a company more than twice as large, with many divisions, more than 100,000 employees, and plants scattered all over the world. Since both companies were clients, I took the occasion to help the new chief executive learn from the more experienced one by guiding the conversation into various aspects of managing. At one point I asked the head of the larger company how he went about making policy.

"I guess I spend more of my time on that than on any other single thing I do," he responded. "We do a lot of fact-finding, even research, when it's a question of an important company-wide policy. We consult the division people. We may get functional specialists and staff people into the act. Then someone will prepare a draft of the policy statement for me to look over.

"I'll look it over and usually prepare a second draft myself. Then I'll circulate my draft to the operating divisions and to any functional department or staff groups that might be involved. In fact, I'll send it not only to people who might be able to make a contribution but to those I want to give a chance to criticize it or just plain squawk before the policy goes into effect.

"When all the suggestions, criticisms, and squawks are in, one of our staff people prepares a third draft. Then I really manicure the words, taking into account the suggestions and criticisms of a few key people whose judgment I value or who should have something special to offer on that particular subject. Finally, we get the necessary approvals and publish the policy in written form, with copies going into our policy guides. And when it goes out, I *know* it will be followed. Our people have been trained that way for years."

The other chief executive, who had been listening attentively, blurted out, "Wow, you're certainly way ahead of us. No wonder you turn in such a good earnings record."

I know other chief executives who "manicure" words when they make policy. They, too, know that policies, standards, and procedures deserve more attention than they commonly get— and have learned that they are effective as guidelines to action and profits when they are carefully made, reduced to writing, and followed.

5

Organization: The Harness to Help People Pull Together

One summer afternoon a friend telephoned me about a golf game. He had a twosome and was looking for two more. I accepted, and we spent a minute discussing whom we might get as the fourth. But we did not settle on anyone. Nor did we decide which of us was to get the fourth.

The next day I met another member of the club. He agreed to join us, and I immediately called my friend with the news. But in the meantime he too had invited a guest, so we had one too many. Since my friend could hardly "disinvite" his guest, I called back the member I had invited and told him of our plight. He was most understanding and readily agreed to withdraw. So no harm was done.

Even so, the incident was embarrassing to me, and it could easily have been avoided. All we had needed to do in our first telephone conversation was to follow one of the most fundamental principles of organization: decide who does what. In more technical terms, we should have fixed on one of us the responsibility for getting the fourth player, and delegated to him the authority to do so.

Importance of Good Organization

Unfortunately, hundreds of organizational muddles of much greater consequence take place every day in even the largest and best-managed companies. Their causes are failure to define who does what, who has what authority, and who reports to whom. The consequences of the resulting mix-ups and conflicts are duplication, wasted effort, delay, frustration, angry words, or relaxing and letting the other fellow do it. And countless mix-ups and conflicts throughout a company combine to bring about ineffective performance, needlessly high costs, loss of competitive position, low morale, reduced profits, and lost opportunities to develop executives. Such results throughout the economy add up to a staggering waste of our national resources. Fortunately, the Communists are even worse at organizing than we are.

Let me recall one more incident that shows the importance of good organization. It concerns an able man in his early thirties whom I often used to meet as we walked to the same commuting train. He was a product manager in a large consumer and industrial goods company.

One morning he told me that he was going to resign his job that day, because he had just accepted a new position with a direct competitor. Naturally, I asked him why he had changed. This was his answer, as accurately as I can remember his words:

"There are usually a lot of reasons for every job change, and I suppose it's hard for even the man himself to know exactly why he did it. In my new job I'll have a better chance to get ahead, and I'll make a little more money. I like the people in the new company. But I like my present people, too. I guess my main reason for taking the new job is the way my present division is organized. As you know, I'm a product

manager. I'm held accountable for profits on my line of products, though I'm only in charge of marketing. But procurement happens to be the principal factor in our division's
profits. So if the procurement people do poorly, I take the rap
—even though I have nothing to say about how they buy or
how much inventory we carry.

"Actually, the chief executive of the whole corporation is
the one really responsible for profits on my line, and my line
is only one tiny part of our total business. I've done my best to
get the setup changed; but all I could get was agreement to let
me handle communications more directly instead of going up
one line to the top and then down the other.

"So I'm going in and break the news to my boss this morning. I plan to tell him the way my job is organized was a major
factor in my leaving. But since I'm going with a direct competitor, they'll probably be so busy getting me out of the place
by noon that the setup point won't register."

That product manager may have been a serious loss to his
company. Far more serious was the loss of one man to General
Motors. Mr. Sloan tells the story:

> As to organization, we did not have adequate knowledge
> or control of the individual operating divisions. It was man-
> agement by crony, with the divisions operating on a horse-
> trading basis. When Walter Chrysler, one of the best men in
> General Motors, became a general executive of the corpora-
> tion, he collided with Mr. Durant over their respective juris-
> dictions, I believe. Mr. Chrysler was a man of strong will and
> feeling. When he could not get the arrangement he wanted, he
> left the corporation. I remember the day. He banged the door
> on the way out, and out of that bang eventually came the
> Chrysler Corporation.[1]

Thus we must add loss of able people to the penalties of poor
organization.

From close observation of the destructive consequences of

inadequate and unsound organization, I am convinced that the will to manage must include the will to organize. Organizing, then, is a managing process that must be part of any effective system of management.

Disdain for Formal Organization

I have also observed, however, that organizing is a much neglected and underrated managing process. In fact, I find that business executives more often have disdain than respect for organizational planning. Here are some typical comments I have heard from high-level executives in sizable companies:

> "We don't go in much for formal organization around here. We're more interested in people than in boxes on charts."

> "Suppose there *is* some confusion. The strong men will always get along all right, and the others we can't worry much about anyway. Even a good dogfight isn't always bad."

> "Formal organization is too restricting. We want every man to feel he can go ahead and do things on his own."

Here is how Ralph Cordiner, then president of General Electric Company, dealt with formal organization structure as a restriction on performance:

> You are familiar with the argument that an organization chart consists of little boxes within which the talents of men are confined and within which their capacity for creative and individual effort is smothered. Certainly you can misuse even a well-defined organization structure to achieve such purposes. But equally certain, you do not need to do so.[2]

By showing the benefits that leading companies have gained from effective organization, I hope to replace with respect any disdain you may have for this managing process. Organizational planning is a really valuable managing tool that should be better understood and more extensively used.

What Organization Really Is

Organizing is a fundamental managing process as old as human history itself. The Bible tells of the advice Moses received from his father-in-law, Jethro. Feeling that Moses was making too many decisions himself in governing his people, Jethro said, "The thing that thou doest is not good. Thou wilt surely wear away, both thou, and this people that is with thee; thou art not able to perform it thyself alone." Moses followed this advice and did a better job of organizing. In the words of the Scripture:

> Moses harkened to the voice of his father-in-law and did all that he said. And Moses chose able men out of all Israel, and made them heads over the people, rulers of thousands, rulers of hundreds, rulers of fifties, rulers of tens. And they judged the people at all seasons: the hard causes they brought unto Moses, but every small matter they judged themselves.[3]

As this passage from the Bible shows, organizing is a *planning* process. In simple terms, organization planning consists of these decision steps:

1. The work or activities to be performed in order to carry out plans are determined. The things to be done or tasks to be performed become *duties*.

2. Then these activities are grouped into positions so they can be assigned to an individual, thus becoming *responsibilities*.

3. Next, *authority* is assigned to each position, conferring on the person holding the position the right to carry out the responsibilities himself or to order others to carry them out.

It is useful to recognize the distinction between authority and power. Power is the ability to get things done—by doing them personally or by commanding or influencing others to do them, with or without authority. A person may have power because he is liked or feared, or because he is respected for his knowledge, judgment, skill, force of personality, seniority, age, or past accomplishments.

Authority, which confers the right to command, helps to build power—to legitimize it. But if a person with authority is not respected, his authority may give him little power.

Power may be exercised without authority, and frequently is. For example, a politically minded individual who lacks the necessary authority may require people to act or refrain from acting by exploiting their fears and weaknesses. And a person acting without authority, of course, does not have to accept responsibility for his actions. So, unless he also has the requisite authority, an executive who recognizes the value of good organization and wants to support the management system is careful not to exercise power derived from seniority or popularity.

4. The next step in organization planning is to determine *authority relationships* among positions—that is, decide who reports to whom and what kind of authority, if any, the holder of each position may exercise. This will ensure that every person knows who his boss is, who his subordinates are, and what type and extent of authority he is subject to and can exercise.

5. Finally, the *personal qualifications* required for superior performance in each position should be decided.

Thus organization planning is concerned—in management jargon—with the duties, responsibilities, authorities, relationships, and personal requirements of positions. This kind of planning harnesses and legitimizes power. It also helps to contain illegitimate power.

Disdainful though many business managers are of this powerful tool for managing, the most successful ones do recognize the usefulness of thinking through and making decisions on the duties, responsibilities, relationships, and personal requirements of the positions needed in managing the company. Ideal organization structures almost always have to be modified because ideal people are not available. But it is better to accept compromises in an ideal plan than not to have an ideal plan to start from. And usually, less compromising is needed than is expected.

To be sure, an organization plan *is* restrictive. In fact, *all* managing processes are restrictive. For their purpose is to guide people's efforts toward effectively attaining the objectives of the group; and, in a sense, all guidance is restrictive. If people are to pull together, rather than work at cross-purposes, some harness is needed—and better a planned harness than a tangled one.

Carrying the harness analogy further, the restrictiveness of the management system depends less on the harness itself than on how tightly the reins are held and how frequently and sharply the whip is used. With a soundly developed system of management and good leadership, high-caliber people will work productively and with zest, despite the restrictions of the organization plan and the other system components.

How Organization Structure Affects Performance

In the early days of his administration, President Kennedy had trouble filling an important position in the State Department. As *The New York Times* said editorially, "The President's difficulty in finding anyone willing and able to take the extremely important post of Assistant Secretary of State for Inter-American Affairs would be ridiculous if it were not so serious." [4] It was reported that about 20 candidates had been considered or approached. The names of two candidates who had actually been offered the post became known, but both re-

jected the job when the chips were down. The *Times* editorial
continued:

> Of the probable reasons for their refusal, the main one is
> the dispersion of authority in the field of Latin-American
> affairs. The State Department's Inter-American Bureau has
> been pushed into the background by the White House "task
> force," headed by Adolf Berle, the two White House aides,
> Richard Goodwin and Arthur Schlesinger, Jr., and—in some
> cases like Cuba—by the C.I.A. As a result the State Depart-
> ment staff has become demoralized. How can President Ken-
> nedy expect anyone of importance to assume a post in such
> conditions? At best it will be one of the most difficult and
> thankless jobs in the Government. . . . Mr. Kennedy will ob-
> tain the right man when he offers him a position of authority
> with a clear line of command from the White House through
> the Secretary of State.

Corporate chief executives who seek to attract able men to
poorly defined positions have the same difficulties as did President Kennedy. In business, as in government or any other field,
able people just don't want jobs with inadequate or unclear
authority. Based on my observations of executives at work, and
on hundreds of confidential interviews with executives at all
levels, it is my conviction than any high-caliber man's effectiveness, job satisfaction, and zest for work—from the time he takes
his first job until he retires—are all vitally affected by the structure of the organization in which he works. And there *is* a
structure, whether it is a haphazard tangle or the product of
a formal plan.

The results of organization planning are pictured in organization charts with their boxes and lines of authority. But organization planning really deals with the actions, ambitions,
emotions, and personal effectiveness of people. Whether or not
the actions of individuals are effectively harnessed to achieve

the purposes of the business largely depends, I believe, on how well the plan of organization is fashioned and how resolutely managers at all levels follow it themselves and require others to do so. The boxes and lines on charts are merely symbols of plans that, as part of the management system, help to require and inspire purposeful, productive decisions and actions.

To further illustrate these points, let's shift from the highest levels of government to the lowest levels of a great hotel in London. Beside each bed at Claridge's is a panel of three call buttons, each marked with a symbol—one for the maid, another for the valet, the third for the waiter. Once I pushed the maid's button and asked for stationery, only to be told that I should buzz for the valet. "We each has our own job, y'know, sir," the maid said. Another time I asked a maid to take away the drink tray. She said, "Will you please buzz for the waiter, sir? He would be upset if I took it away."

Organizational planning is a managing process designed for managing people as they are—with all their fine qualities and their meannesses as well. Maids, waiters, product managers, Walter Chryslers, and candidates for Assistant Secretary of State all have their pride. Each wants his own clearly defined job; none wants anyone else interfering with his authority.

A well-planned structure, therefore, is one of the best ways to hold personal politics and personality conflicts in check. Take the Eisenhower Administration's efforts to establish a unified organization for military research and engineering. Again, the Administration had difficulty in finding an outstanding person to accept a post—this time, that of Director of Research and Engineering for the Defense Department. As *The New York Times* reported:

> Authoritative sources made clear today that no one of suitable stature desired the post. One of the reasons, it is said, is

that although the job sounds important, its holder would be helplessly entangled in conflicting lines of authority.

In addition, Pentagon observers feel that few qualified men want to take on the "vested interest" of the military services in their development programs. "Every time anyone suggests a change or coordinated effort at the Pentagon, at least one of the services and usually all of them claim that the change will damage national security," said one official. "The result is a flare-up of infighting in which the generals are far more effective than transplanted educators and business executives," this official added.[5]

Even a perfect organization plan won't control all the imperfections of human nature. But a defective plan can be counted on to bring out the worst in people and to raise costly havoc in the organization. Business executives, like generals and educators, often engage in "infighting." And business concerns, like all other organizations, have their political camps and cliques. These reflections of the mean side of human nature frequently originate from a defective organization structure. At least, such a structure stimulates and facilitates infighting and politics.

Organization Guidelines

Since this is not a technical book, I do not want to go too deeply into the techniques of organization planning. Any reader who wants to know more about techniques can refer to the books and articles listed in the bibliography. But I do want to illustrate a few basic principles or guidelines for organization planning. This will show how simple the process really is. And I hope it will help any executive with the will to manage to detect and correct organization deficiencies more easily and so to gain the many profit-building benefits of good organization.

The so-called "principles of organization" have nothing like the proven validity of natural laws. In fact, management authorities still differ among themselves on many of these. So I feel that they are better termed "guidelines"—guidelines that have emerged from observation and analysis of how people really act in groups.

These guidelines, deeply rooted in both human nature and common sense, spring directly from the nature of the organizational planning process itself. Consequently, I find it most useful to group them according to the basic steps involved in organizational planning. A brief discussion of the guidelines for taking each of these steps will show how to go about the task of establishing an effective organization structure.

■ *Setting up positions:* "A square peg in a round hole" is the cliché often used to describe the man who has failed to perform well in a job. Classic examples are the star salesman who fails as a district sales manager and the outstanding worker who makes a poor foreman. The business losses and the personal heartbreaks that flow from such failures constitute a great waste to the nation. Often the failures are not the fault of the man but of poor organizational decisions by management. And often they can be avoided if senior executives understand and follow the elementary guidelines for setting up positions.

The organizing process is basically one of assigning work to people. Consequently, organization planning starts with deciding what activities are necessary and then grouping the work— by *type* and *amount*—so that the position or job constitutes an assignment that can be performed effectively by an individual.

There are guidelines for making a position "do-able." Basically the different *types* of work (activities) assigned to any position should not be so numerous that it will be hard to fill. That is, the work should be homogeneous enough so there will generally be enough candidates to fill and refill the position without much difficulty. Since most people do not have a wide range of abilities, a position calling for an unusual spread of abilities should ordinarily be avoided. Even if an unusual person is currently available to fill a poorly set-up position, replacements will be difficult to develop, and unnecessary reorganization and upset are likely to result.

The different types of work can be most usefully classified in terms of the personal qualifications needed to perform each type well:

■ *Operating work* is generally repetitive and requires *doing* rather than planning. Therefore, it demands a relatively lower degree of imagination and analytical power.

■ *Analytical work,* such as staff work performed by engineers, and market and financial analysts, calls for highly developed analytical and problem-solving skills. Planning work too requires analytical ability.

■ *Technical work* calls for knowledge of some specialized field, such as engineering, chemistry, accounting, operations research, or electronic data processing. This knowledge must be gained through education and/or job experience.

■ *Creative work,* such as scientific research or advertising, requires a high degree of imagination, vision, and idea-getting ability.

■ *Administrative work,* from the district sales manager's or foreman's job on up, requires knowledge of how to exercise authority and the capacity to direct and get things done through others.

■ *Leadership work,* such as that of the president and the director of marketing, requires the capacity to inspire others to effective performance.

Even at lower levels, positions can usually combine two or more basic types of work. The higher the position, the more varied can be the types of work assigned to it, because fewer people will be needed to fill these positions. A highly creative person will usually dislike routine, and rare skills will be wasted; a man who is good at operating activities will not necessarily be a good analyst, administrator, or leader. Thus, a position entailing several different types of work is less likely to be filled effectively by a given individual. Also, the number of qualified candidates decreases as the range of work assigned to a position increases.

As mentioned earlier, the proportions of time spent on different types of work should shift with the level of the position. You may recall my saying that the chief executive's position ideally involves a minimum of operating activities and a maximum of analytical, creative, administrative, and leadership work.

The guidelines for determining how much work to assign to a position are inherently less specific. If the proper *types* of work are assigned to a position, the person filling it will be able to turn out *more* work. The amount of work to assign to a properly set up position can best be determined from observation by line managers, assisted by specialists such as organization analysts and industrial engineers. Also, by experimentally varying the number of similar positions, the right balance between output and cost can be achieved.

Any executive seeking organizational improvement should consider the possibility of payoff from setting up sound new positions—both line and staff. In expanding sales volume and controlling operations and costs, American companies typically use more specialized staff positions than European companies. When I asked one United States chief executive how he had stepped up profits so sharply, he quipped: "We doubled a low overhead and cut a large cost base in two."

Before creating new positions, however, their hidden costs should be weighed as well as the added salaries. The added bill for supplementary compensation (pension, insurance, hospitalization, etc.) should be specifically totaled. So should the costs of office space and secretarial help. Frequently overlooked as a cost is the difficulty of eliminating a position that proves to be unprofitable: The incumbent and his immediate associates will strongly resist the move, and their arguments may be difficult to refute.

Consequently, effective organization planning also challenges the value of existing positions as well as setting up new ones. The simple question, "Is this work necessary?" may result in eliminating activities or even entire positions. An activity that once was necessary may become obsolete as conditions change. For example, technical services established during a new-product introduction may not be necessary after the product is well established. In business, the will to manage does not permit the luxury of vested interests.

■ *Granting authority.* No position can be soundly set up unless its holder has the authority necessary to carry out his duties or responsibilities. This requirement can be most easily met if one well-established organization principle (or guideline) is followed throughout the business: Responsibility and authority should go hand in hand. This, of course, simply means that when responsibilities are assigned to a position, everyone understands that the holder of the position has the necessary authority to carry them out. This concept is a powerful instrument for making the will to manage effective.

Many companies, both large and small, go well beyond that broad way of granting authority. Most commonly, they incorporate in written job descriptions various specific grants of authority: approving capital investment, granting salary

increases, hiring people at various levels of salary, signing contracts, retaining lawyers and consultants, etc.

There are two types of authority: line and functional. In
building a system of management, both should be understood
and used. Let me get a little technical for just a few pages.
There is a big payoff from using these two types of authority
properly and from understanding the difference between functional authority and staff work.

Line authority, the commonest and best-understood type
of authority, gives an executive the right to command or give
direct orders to subordinates. The line executive controls his
subordinates chiefly through discipline (approval or disapproval) and decisions or recommendations on compensation
or promotion. His ultimate control, of course, is the right to
hire and fire. Awareness of the superior's right to fire is the
most powerful negative control in any system of management.

The line executive is concerned with determining the
need, time, and place for action and with issuing direct orders
to line subordinates to get things done. He says "Do it," and
"Do it *now.*" It is line authority that goes hand in hand with
responsibility.

Line authority extends directly from the chief executive
of a business, through the various levels of authority, to the
lowest level of operating or sales supervisor who directs any
subordinates. In the United States military establishment, the
President as Commander-in-Chief has a direct line of authority
down to every squad leader or crew chief of every American
military unit anywhere in the world.

That is all pretty clear and not very technical. But let's
turn now to functional authority.

The concept of functional authority is more subtle than
that of line authority. It is also less widely understood and

used. Yet proper understanding and use of this concept can be of great value in a company of any size. And as companies become larger, more complex, and more subject to the impact of rapid change, its usefulness grows.

Functional authority (sometimes called technical authority) is simply the right to see that activities carried on in other departments or other organizational units are conducted in accordance with the requirements of the department or organizational unit that has functional (or technical) authority. Functional authority has its origin in the greater technical or specialized knowledge of the executive, department, or unit that exercises it.

If line authority is a grant of power, functional authority is the authority of knowledge. Just as the holder of line authority says "Do it," and "Do it *now,*" the holder of functional authority says, "If and when you do it, do it this way—or in accordance with this policy or standard."

Perhaps the meaning of functional *authority* can best be clarified by examples:

1. The controller has functional authority over all accounting procedures throughout the business. He prescribes how transactions shall be recorded, and line executives must follow his instructions.

2. The purchasing department sets standards for local purchases made by line departments. If and when they buy parts, supplies, or materials, they must buy to established standards.

3. The personnel department has functional authority to prescribe to line executives how grievances shall be handled, what salary ranges shall be used, what limitations there may be on dismissals, etc.

4. The public relations department prescribes restrictions and guidelines on what plant managers shall discuss with the local press and how they shall discuss it.

These illustrations point up another important aspect of the functional authority concept: Line executives help enforce *functional* authority by putting their line authority behind it. The chief executive, in effect, orders all line executives to follow and enforce the policies, procedures, and standards of the functional departments. Thus, the functional departments are not merely advisory. They have their own authority, which is backed by line authority. Nor, as we shall see, are functional departments the same as staff departments.

Functional departments should approach the job of enforcing their policies, standards, and procedures in a spirit of exercising authority, not just offering advice. Their work will then be more useful and more responsible, and the resulting guidelines are more likely to be followed. That does not mean, of course, that functional departments should be arrogant in exercising authority. Indeed, the most effective functional departments seldom need to resort to a show of authority. Their policies, standards, and procedures should be so useful, so sensible, and so persuasively presented that the line departments will be glad to follow and enforce them.

If a line department disagrees with a policy, standard, or procedure established by a functional department, and the difference of opinion cannot be resolved, it is referred to the next highest common *line* superior of the executives who differ. For example, a plant manager may disagree with the plant controller, who reports to him but is required to enforce the procedures established in the company controller's department. The plant manager first tries to persuade the plant controller. If that fails, they refer the issue to their respective line and functional superiors, who seek to resolve the issue through discussion. The final decision is made by the highest common line superior to whom the issue can be appealed—perhaps even the chief executive.

This system of checks and balances is of great value in bringing about the best compromise between getting things done quickly and getting them done right—i.e., in accordance with company policies, standards, and philosophy. An over-zealous functional executive cannot long hold up important operations that may conflict with a functional policy, standard, or procedure. This is because line executives always have the opportunity to convince functional executives or line superiors that the functional guideline is wrong and should be changed, or that an exception should be made in this instance. Thus, the balance between line and functional authority is an important means for developing and requiring adherence to a system of management that makes the will to manage effective.

Parenthetically, a company philosophy that includes an objective, factual approach to resolving issues permits the best use of the checks and balances between line and functional authority. Under such a philosophy, people will try to determine *what* is right, not *who* is right. Persuasion based on facts is more effective. In the light of new facts people can change their positions with less damage to their pride. Issues can be resolved in a factual atmosphere with fewer injured feelings, less "showing the other guy," and fewer I-told-you-so's.

Most functional executives also have line authority. For example, the controller and top purchasing, personnel administration, and public relations executives all have line authority over personnel in their own departments.

Here, then, is a summary of the values of developing an understanding of functional authority in a company and putting the concept to work:

■ Functional authority provides an effective means of making technical and specialized knowledge more productive in a company. The functional executive who develops sound poli-

cies, standards, and procedures on the basis of technical kn
edge and proper study and analysis also has the authority tu
make them effective. The importance of this advantage will
grow as science, technology, and advanced knowledge of all
types become increasingly important to business success. Functional specialists with authority are better able to help their
companies cope with and capitalize on change.

▪ With proper functional authority, specialists and tech-
nicians need not feel like second-class citizens, entirely dependent on their powers of persuasion. At the same time, their
knowledge of the checks that line executives can impose on
them should keep them from being officious and arrogant—
if common sense does not. Consequently, a company in which
functional authority is recognized can more easily attract and
retain the knowledgeable specialists that every company needs
in a complex environment of rapid technological change.

▪ The system of checks and balances, by providing for
appeals up the line, ensures that the line executives are always
in command on major issues. The chief executive has the
security of knowing that line executives, who are ultimately
responsible for profits, can assert their line authority any time
they wish. And he knows that issues of enough importance will
ultimately be appealed to him if they cannot be resolved at a
lower level.

▪ Recognition and exercise of functional authority can
provide any company with a powerful competitive advantage
by identifying *ideas* that have value and making sure that they
are put to work. I can think of three outstanding companies
that owe their success largely to distinctive personnel policies
and programs, thought through by personnel executives and
made effective through exercise of recognized functional authority. In all three companies the line executives came to

recognize the values of these policies and now enforce them eagerly.

In many industries competition is so keen that only *idea generation* and *management effectiveness* can provide the competitive edge. We have seen how functional authority can help increase management effectiveness. It can help idea generation, too. A strong functional department helps to attract men of ideas. And with functional authority behind their ideas, they can get these ideas—in the form of distinctive and highly relevant policies—right into the company's bloodstream.

I have discussed functional authority at this length because I believe that it offers real competitive advantage to any company that will make the effort and take the time to build the concept into its system of management. Let's turn now to a brief discussion of staff work and clinch this understanding of the functional authority concept.

Staff activity, properly understood, consists simply of fact-finding, analysis, and the development of advice and recommendations. Unlike a functional department, a staff unit—market research, engineering, legal—*has no authority;* it is purely advisory. A staff unit cannot *enforce* its recommendations, however valuable they may be. Staff people can only advise and persuade; line or functional departments receiving this advice may act on it or ignore it, as they choose.

The term "staff" is commonly used to cover all activities that are not clearly line work, thus blurring or obliterating the concept of functional authority. This fuzziness is unfortunate because it forecloses an opportunity for competitive advantage.

The persuasiveness of its personnel is therefore an important factor in the success of a staff unit. However, if a fact-founded philosophy is adhered to, facts will carry more weight and less burden will fall on personal persuasion. Moreover, when the higher-level executives in a well-managed company accept staff advice, they let it be known that others should do so too.

In several companies that have given specific attention to building management systems, staff-department services are charged to the using department. The staff units are expected to make their services so valuable that they develop a line "clientele." Du Pont's engineering department, for example, publishes a booklet to tell executives in the operating departments about the services it has to offer.

The difference between a staff and a functional unit is inherent in the kind of work they do. Some types of activity require technical *authority* and cannot depend solely on advice and recommendation. Whether a particular unit has functional authority is determined by the chief executive. With written job descriptions, that determination can be easily made.

Although staff activities have grown greatly in U.S. companies during the past 25 years, further growth is needed to cope with the growing size and complexity of companies and with changes in the business environment. Desirable new staff units—such as strategic planning, logistics, and organization planning—will meet with less fear and resistance, and hence are more likely to be successfully established, if it is clear that they are strictly advisory. Thus the forces at work—both external and internal—can be better coped with and capitalized on through increased staff work.

The "Office" Concept in Organizing

Establishing the concept that each major position is an *office* will help substantially to transmit the will to manage throughout the company and make it effective in action. This concept is simple, subtle, and useful. It merely means recognizing each position as a bundle of responsibility and authority, distinct from the person who holds it. The incumbent *fills* the office—he does not *make* it.

As it applies to the Presidency of the United States, this concept is well accepted and broadly understood. That office is recognized as something apart from and bigger than the man who currently holds it, as indicated by the common phrase "respect for the office." Because of the great authority and power of the Presidency, the man who fills it usually seeks to measure up to the country's expectations. Frequently a man of limited stature surprises everyone, including himself, by the way he does fill the *office*.

In most business concerns, much the same concept applies to the office of chief executive. The chief executive expands or contracts the authority of his office. In the way he carves out the scope and performs the job, people throughout the company come to understand, accept, and expect that the job will be performed that way, and a very real image of the *office* of chief executive is built up in people's minds. They act and react accordingly. This concept can be a useful, even powerful, part of a management system if top management understands it and acts to build "offices" at all levels possible.

In one very large corporation, for example, the president was a very dominant individual—a poor delegator but a brilliant and successful decision maker. His successor, on taking over the presidency, was staggered by the number of issues brought to him for decision. He was even more dismayed by the way people hung on his words and reacted to any indication of his opinion as if it were a command. I pointed out to him that the people in the business had simply come to accept the "office" of president as it had been built by his predecessor.

I advised him to rebuild the office by gradually delegating more authority and making certain that his subordinates, instead of trying to anticipate his wishes, waited for him to analyze the facts, state his conclusions, and announce his decisions. After about 3 years, the office of president in his company was changed in "size," but it was still an *office*.

In most companies, unfortunately, positions are not widely enough recognized at lower levels as *offices*. As a rule, every senior position has some acceptance and recognition as an office, but too often each executive below the chief executive must do too much building of the position himself. Frequently new incumbents are obliged to do battle with other executives to establish authority that clearly should attach to the position, not the man. In companies with *personal* management, the authorities of the position are, in effect, expanded or contracted from week to week, or even from day to day, as the incumbent gains or loses personal standing with those above him whose power has been established.

Lack of established "offices" makes for a continuing power struggle. As new people enter positions, the others involved wait to see how much support each new executive gets from higher up. Not only are such struggles wasteful; they usually permit the politician to get power that should not go with the "office." And when a struggle for power or standing gets extreme, the more capable executives will leave, because they don't want to work in an atmosphere of insecurity that keeps them busy thinking about where they stand.

Consequently, part of building a system of management is to build respect for the office at all possible levels of management. This is done in the ways I have discussed: by defining the responsibilities and authorities of each position, and by making it clear that "the way we do things around here" re-

quires every executive—from the chief executive on down—
to build positions and develop men to fill them.

Each executive does this "building" by holding his subordinates accountable for the responsibilities of the position,
and supporting them in the exercise of the authorities that
attach to the position. He should, of course, make it clear to
all concerned that he is supporting the authority of the *position,* not the executive as an individual. This approach makes
for personal security, minimizes personal and corporate politics, improves performance, and builds esprit.

Staffing the Structure

I have already discussed the usefulness of defining the ideal
structure and job content of each position and the ideal
qualifications of the person to fill it. That may be termed a
theoretical approach—and it is. But it is in the effort to achieve
the ideal that the great practical value of this approach lies.

Modifying the ideal structure to fit the available people
comes almost too naturally in most situations. Unusual responsibilities may be attached to a position because the incumbent has specialized abilities. Again, two jobs may be
combined to fit the unusually broad abilities of a particular
individual. Or the responsibilities of a position may be nar-
rowed down because the individual who holds it does not have
all of the abilities it really requires. In these circumstances,
not all the work gets done and part of the "office" just atro-
phies.

But these and other types of modifications are an inherent
part of organization planning, since ideal individuals are almost never available. Nevertheless, efforts to achieve the ideal
are truly worthwhile, because people will usually stretch themselves to fill the position to which they have been assigned.

Moreover, those who are selecting people to fill positions will do better if they are working against ideal specifications.

I cannot over-stress the value of ideal specifications as the basis for selecting people for positions. I recall the case of a chairman and president who were faced with the task of picking a man to move into the presidency when the chairman retired and the president moved up to chairman. There were three outstanding candidates. As they discussed the selection with me, I realized that they were about to reach agreement on one of the three—not, in my opinion, the best-qualified one. I asked them to let me prepare a memorandum outlining the important management problems the president would face during the next 10 years, and the personal qualifications he would need for the job.

After a couple of drafts, we reached agreement in writing on the character of the job and personal qualifications needed to fill it well. Then the chairman and the president separately evaluated the three candidates in terms of those qualifications. They quickly reached agreement on a man whom they had been on the point of passing over. He proved to be an excellent choice, and the company has prospered handsomely under his leadership.

Whether the position is that of district sales manager, foreman, or president, the same approach should be followed: Set up a definite position, specify the types of work included in the position, define the ideal qualifications of the individual to perform those types of work well, analyze the personal qualifications of each candidate on the basis of his demonstrated performance, and then match the qualifications for the job to those of the candidates as well as possible.

This approach enforces objectivity and leads those making the selection to consider more candidates in an effort to find the man who meets the ideal specifications. Let me illustrate its value with another example. In selecting a chief executive of a large company, the nonexecutive directors developed a memorandum that spelled out the qualifications they sought in the next chief executive. It contained this statement:

> The directors recognize that these qualities characterize the "ideal" man (who does not exist), but we wish nevertheless to evaluate each candidate against these qualifications before making the choice, by balancing the strengths and inevitable shortcomings of the various candidates. Specifically, we believe we will make a better choice by starting with a set of ideal qualifications rather than by starting with less.

This approach works just that way: those selecting an individual for a position will make a better choice if they start with a set of ideal qualifications rather than merely a vague notion of what sort of man is needed to do the job effectively. This approach also enables objective selectors to deal better with others who are anxious to choose a friend or someone to whom they are obligated. It is the fact-founded approach applied to job selection.

The Board of Directors

Two common complaints of chief executives are the difficulty of staffing the board of directors and the difficulty of getting effective performance from it. Capable directors are hard to find and hard to interest in the position. And many chief executives find the board's performance disappointing. These complaints are serious, because an effective board is an important element in any system of management. The whole subject of the board of directors is too broad to treat here, but I want to comment on these two specific complaints because I believe they are interrelated.

Staffing the board: Good directors are hard to get for two principal reasons. First, only a few companies make an organized effort to recruit them. Those that do usually determine well in advance the qualifications they want in directors and identify individuals who fulfill the requirements. When a vacancy occurs, they are then in a position to approach several candidates in a predetermined order of priority. In some companies the recruiting program is not only well organized, but specifically assigned to a high-level executive. Most companies, however, are too haphazard in recruiting directors.

Second, directors are usually given inadequate incentives to serve. Some companies pay their directors larger fees—thus making the position financially more attractive—and expect more work. But money is often not a good incentive because many desirable directors, especially for large companies, are in such high tax brackets that bigger fees make little difference in their after-tax earnings.

For most directors, there are better incentives than money. Well-managed companies can offer directors who are executives in other companies attractive opportunities to learn from their management practices and to get specific background and help from staff and operating departments. Thus the company with an effective programmed management system has an attractive incentive for other executives to devote time to the board. Moreover, the well-managed business has a better chance of attracting capable directors to begin with. Not only does the position offer greater prestige, but the individuals approached know they will be less likely to be faced with unpleasant issues and tough decisions concerning executive performance.

Companies are learning that they can "trade" directors. For example, General Foods and Gillette each have a high-level executive on the other's board. Through their directors, these two well-managed, noncompeting companies can each learn much from the management practices and operations of the other.

Many men lack incentive to join a board, or lose interest once they have joined, because the chief executive does not ask them or allow them to direct. Naturally, most directors don't want to ask, much less insist, that they be permitted to do their jobs. Capable individuals who serve as directors want real involvement. They want to know what is going on; they want a real voice in establishing major policies, selecting top executives, and appraising performance. They want responsibility and challenge. By providing these incentives for the individual director, the chief executive will get better performance from the board as a whole.

In summary, then, the chief executive who has difficulty in attracting capable directors should examine the company's director recruiting program and the nonfinancial incentives it offers. In my experience, a well-managed business with a well-organized director recruiting program usually has little difficulty in attracting capable directors.

Board performance: The chief executive who is dissatisfied with his board's performance had better look first at the way he is using the board. The board is, or should be, an independent body that—among other things—selects the chief executive and appraises his performance. The capable chief executive gives the directors the basis for providing him with critical evaluation and help—he lets them know he expects and welcomes it. This makes the directors' job more interesting as well as more productive.

Too many chief executives fail to get full value from capable directors, simply because they don't ask for their help.

Capable directors are disappointed by superficial board meetings and resent being used as rubber stamps. There is the quip about the directors of a large company with a dominant and domineering chief executive: If you see a group of men walking along the hall with their heads bobbing up and down, it's just the directors on their way to a board meeting, practicing to yes the chief executive.

If the chief executive does call on his board properly and still doesn't get good performance, then the deficiencies probably lie with the individuals themselves, the time they give to board work, or the interest they have in the company. Directors who don't direct should resign or be replaced. They are a menace to the free enterprise system. Their neglect of their duty to stockholders opens the company to raids, take-overs, and proxy fights, soundly or unsoundly motivated. And, of course, extreme dereliction of duty exposes directors to personal lawsuits.

The Chief Executive

Most of the chief executive's responsibilities are fairly well recognized: making final decisions on major issues, approving high-level personnel selections and compensation, obtaining board approval for actions and decisions beyond the chief executive's authority, and the like. But other important responsibilities of the position are often overlooked by chief executives themselves, as well as by the directors who select the chief executive, aid him in his work, and review his performance.

When Gardner Cowles announced in May 1964 that he was relinquishing the presidency of Cowles Magazines & Broadcasting, Inc. (publisher of *Look* magazine), but continuing as chairman and chief executive officer, he said:

This change was made by the board of directors at my request. It does not mean that I expect to work any less hard. I do hope, however, to be able to give more personal attention to long-range planning and to have more time to devote to possible acquisitions.[6]

Clearly, Mr. Cowles felt the need to devote more time to what I have called "strategic planning." He was recognizing more fully a responsibility that many chief executives under-emphasize and even neglect: serving as chief architect of corporate strategy. As discussed earlier, strategic plans are those that determine the kind of business, where it is going, and how it is going to get there in the face of competition. The responsibility and initiative for strategic planning rest with the chief executive.

The chief executive may not develop strategic plans himself, but he should be sensitive to their importance and see to it that they are developed and implemented. He must, for example, direct the company so as to cope with increasing competition on an international scale and with rapid technological, political, and social change. And since continuing success requires growth, he must prepare it to cope with the problems of ever-increasing size and complexity.

The chief executive of a successful business is also the chief architect of the company's system of management. And after the system is built, he must articulate it and see that it is used, supported, and revised as changing conditions require.

Thus, I believe that any chief executive will do a better job if he thinks of himself not only as leader and final decision maker but also as an architect with two broad responsibilities: (1) keeping the company attuned to external forces, and (2) building and maintaining a system of management. Company success will increasingly require a chief executive who is a conceptual thinker—that is, who can convert ideas, particulars, and specifics into notions or principles of broad applicability. Under current and future conditions, the ideal chief executive is a man of ideas as well as a man of action.

The chief executive is also chief personnel officer for the executive and supervisory staff. It is his responsibility to see that there is a sufficient intake of high-caliber talent; that this talent is properly developed, compensated, and advanced; and that personnel standards are adhered to. These responsibilities are discussed in the next chapter.

The chief executive is, of course, the company's leader. In carrying out that responsibility, he sets an example by adhering to the company's management system himself, and he inspires and requires others to do likewise. In fact, one of the great advantages of a management system, as we will see in Chapter 8, is that it provides leadership "leverage" that makes it easier for any chief executive to be an effective leader.

In observing the performance of chief executives, I have noticed that the most outstanding have another common denominator: They *seek out* major problems, especially difficult executive personnel problems, and either solve them or find some other way of dealing with them. Weak chief executives, on the other hand, tend to avoid difficult problems and hope that they will go away. (Usually, of course, they get more serious.)

Even when a problem can be better dealt with later on, or actually solved by the passage of time, the strong chief executive will specifically determine that that is the solution and will see to it that the proper people understand how the problem will be handled. This approach strengthens the confidence of company personnel in his leadership, because they know he is not ducking a tough problem.

In summary, my observations convince me that the difference between good and outstanding performance by a chief executive depends largely on how well he performs the following major responsibilities—*responsibilities for which the initiative rests with him:*

- Developing strategic plans, including identifying major opportunities and seeing that they are seized
- Designing the management system
- Directing executive personnel management
- Adhering to the system of management himself and seeing that it is followed by others
- Seeking out major problems and seeing that they are solved or otherwise dealt with
- Providing "let's go" leadership (discussed in the last chapter).

Decentralization and Recentralization

Establishment of the operating division—one of the outstanding management phenomena of the past four decades—has given great impetus to decentralization of responsibility and authority in American business. Pioneered by Du Pont and General Motors, the trend to set up separate operating divisions gained new momentum during the past two decades from the outstandingly successful decentralization of General Electric, carried out under the leadership of Ralph Cordiner. Some students of management assert that the growing use of computers will slow or reverse that trend.

The basic reason for establishing an operating division is to provide a better means for managing what is essentially a distinct kind of business. That is why most operating divisions are built around discrete products or groups of products. Establishment of the separate unit permits the people involved to concentrate their interest and attention, and to have direct responsibility for a "business within a business." In fact, the managements of the most successful divisionalized companies I have studied go to extremes to avoid interfering with the division management's accountability for results.

Therefore, I am convinced that the computer should not be permitted to reverse or even slow the trend toward delegation and divisionalization. A wise management will not allow the computer to interfere with delegation of authority to divisions or within divisions.

The computer is an extraordinary information tool with an extraordinary impact on business generally, including organization structure. But it *is* an information tool. Its function is to provide information that could not previously be obtained, or could not be obtained as accurately or as fast. By enabling management to obtain information about the relative attractiveness of different decision alternatives, the computer improves the quality of decision making. All this information is more readily available at the top of any company or division, and facilitates centralized decision making.

But lack of adequate information is only one reason for delegation and divisionalization—and it is not the principal one. Recentralization of decision making at a level above the general manager of a division will reduce the accountability of the division. It will narrow the possibilities of interdivisional competition, reduce the effectiveness of division profit as a measure of performance and a basis for incentive, and restrict the development of people who make decisions at lower levels.

For these reasons, I believe that corporate executives above the division level—as well as executives within the division—should resist the temptation to use computer-provided information in making decisions for lower-level executives.

Reorganizing

One of the large tobacco companies once built a high-impact advertising campaign for cigars around the slogan, "Spit is a horrid word." In most companies, "reorganization" is a horrid word—but it shouldn't be.

Reorganization is feared because it brings change—and people generally abhor change of any kind. The changes associated with reorganization are especially "horrid" because of their assumed effects on job security. People can even get fired. The very word "reorganization" has acquired a negative connotation from being used in announcements that do involve violent change, including loss of jobs. Such announcements receive the greatest publicity when the company or division in question is unprofitable, for changes in organization structure and job assignments are often necessary to convert losses into profits.

In point of fact, *reorganizing* is synonymous with *organizing*, except that it is *re*planning instead of an initial planning of activities. Reorganizing is much less "horrid" if approached in this way. And this is the way any business *should* approach the managing process of organizational planning to cope with change.

In a growing, successful business, there ought to be frequent reorganization. To accommodate or facilitate more extensive or complex activities, new positions must be added and existing positions changed. One mark of sophisticated and successful management is high tolerance for change and reorganization among executives and supervisors. In a successful, growing business, in fact, organizational changes should come to be regarded as routine.

To be sure, I can think of several successful companies

that make organizational changes too frequently. Because they have a high tolerance for change, fear (which does exist) is not serious. But the constant upsetting of normal operating routines keeps the people whose positions are directly affected from learning their jobs, reduces effectiveness, and adds to costs. For every violent change cuts the "arteries and nerves" of working relationships between people who have gotten used to each other; and new relationships must be established.

Of course, skill in management calls for striking a nice balance between change that keeps the business organizationally up to date or even a little ahead, and change so violent or so frequent as to keep people in a state of doubt, indecision, and ferment. After any substantial organizational change, people need time to settle down and learn how the new structure and people work. Like a good golf swing, an administrative organization should become sufficiently "grooved" so that people can go about their work without having to think about who does what.

Thus, with a continuous, properly paced updating of organization structure, reorganization will be recognized as a normal, even routine, element in a programmed management system.

Organization for Organizing

Since organization planning is an important management process and an essential component of the programmed management system, any large company or division needs a special staff unit to do organization planning. Such a unit can range from a single individual, working part time, to a staff of half-a-dozen people.

It is essential that the staff man or the head of the organization planning unit be someone who enjoys the confidence and support of the chief executive. He should report directly to the chief executive or one of his immediate subordinates.

The staff head needs no special experience. He should be a person whom people trust and in whom they feel they can confide. Given intelligence, analytical ability, imagination, and common sense, he can learn organization planning by doing it and studying texts on the side—starting, perhaps, with those listed in the bibliography.

You've no doubt seen the popular cartoon about organizing that has been reproduced on ash trays. Two men are virtually lying down in their chairs, with their feet on a long, low table. The caption is, "Tomorrow we've got to get organized."

Many companies do put off "getting organized." But the successful ones recognize organizational planning as a specialized activity that can contribute importantly to success. Neglected though it often is, organization planning provides another "secret weapon" that any company can put into its success arsenal.

6

Executive Personnel Administration: Developing the Primary Resource of the Business

Some years ago I had dinner with the late Branch Rickey, then general manager of the Brooklyn Dodgers. Mr. Rickey was then at the peak of acclaim for having converted the Dodgers from a miserably performing baseball club into regular contenders for the National League pennant. The purpose of our get-together was to give him some background for a speech he was to make to the Harvard Business School Club of New York, of which I was then president.

As a student of management I had long felt there was much to be learned about executive personnel management from the way managers in professional sports, especially baseball and football, handled their personnel. And from reading the sports pages, I felt sure Branch Rickey had developed concepts that could be applied to all types of businesses. Our dinner together, and the speech he made later, confirmed this.

During his successful career with the St. Louis Cardinals, Mr. Rickey had pioneered the farm system—a network of subsidiary minor league clubs that hire and train untried players so that the most talented can be advanced to the parent major league club.

At dinner that night Mr. Rickey said: "What I look for in a ball player is speed, a good throwing arm, a sharp batting eye, and intelligence. Given these abilities and a determination to succeed, we can make good ball players out of a high proportion of our raw material. A few will become stars."

This is both a surer and more profitable way to manage a baseball business than buying proven players from other clubs, Mr. Rickey went on. Young, inexperienced players are paid less, and they can be advanced gradually as they prove themselves. The system provides depth of talent and any excess can be sold off. Developed in St. Louis, the system had also worked well in Brooklyn. Now, of course, it is common practice in both leagues.

Another comment on the importance of capable players to success in baseball appeared in a column by Joe Williams, noted sports reporter for the Scripps-Howard newspapers:

> Beginning October 1, the Detroit Tigers are to operate under new management. Fred Knorr, a local radio executive, is to function as president. It's been more than 10 years since the Tigers won. Mr. Knorr thinks he has a wonderful recovery idea. "Next season we'll have a fiery, active manager who will inspire the players and get out there on the field and fight for them. . . ." *In due course, Mr. Knorr will discover, as did many who came before him, that managers, whether they think with their larynx or their head, are successful in almost exact ratio to the caliber of the talent at their command.*[1]

Executive Personnel Administration as a System Component

From observations behind the scenes of successful companies, I am convinced that what Mr. Williams said of baseball is just as true of business. In stating what may on the surface seem obvious, I would paraphrase his statement only slightly: "Success in business is in almost exact ratio to the caliber of executive talent at top management's command."

That is why administration of executive personnel is a key component of a successful management system—and why I believe that a company's basic strategy should be designed and carried out so as to attract, retain, and motivate high-caliber executive talent. Moreover, the interactions between this and other system components are critical to success in managing high-caliber executive talent.

The mere fact that it is on the payroll, however, does not mean that executive talent is at the effective command of top management. To be *effectively* at top management's command, it must be working *productively*. And full productivity means that the executives are purposeful, effective, and reasonably enthusiastic in whatever they think, decide, and do. In those terms, every other system component also influences executive productivity.

The "crunch" of any management system is on the executive firing line. To make the will to manage really effective, therefore, the system of management must (1) provide *enough* executive talent, (2) put that talent into the *right* jobs, and (3) make each individual executive *productive* in his work. In meeting these system requirements, five major elements of executive personnel management must be adequately provided for:

- Planning executive manpower needs
- Recruiting and selecting enough high-caliber executive trainee candidates
- Developing trainees and executives for better performance and for advancement to higher positions
- Advancing executives and trainees to higher positions, and getting rid of the poor performers

- Compensating executives in ways that will stimulate their productivity.

Some years ago, in preparing an article for the *Harvard Business Review*, I made a survey of high-talent manpower. Some 1,900 anonymous questionnaires were mailed out, chiefly to alumni of six leading graduate business schools employed in large companies. About 600 responded, in most cases with extensive comments. The results confirmed a number of conclusions I had drawn from discussions with high-talent men over the years, and I draw on that high-talent survey in discussing the five major elements.

Executive Manpower Planning

In 1955, the Cleveland Browns won their second straight National League professional football championship. This win followed ten straight divisional crowns and was the seventh play-off victory in those ten years. Speaking in Cleveland after winning that championship, Paul Brown, coach and general manager of the Browns, said: "The underlying reason why we've been on top is that these are basically high-class people." And Arthur Daley, in his *New York Times* column, remarked of Mr. Brown: "No football coach—or baseball manager, for that matter—is one bit better than his material. The resourceful Paul has made sure he'd have the right personnel through long-range planning." [2]

Every top-management corporate executive would readily agree that executive material is just as important to success in business—and that long-range planning is just as necessary. Yet my observations show that most companies—including even the well-managed ones—can do more specific and more effective executive manpower planning. And this is likelier to happen if executive manpower planning is approached strategically, as part of a management system.

In one of the largest and most successful U.S. businesses—a company that does *not* slight these fundamentals—the chief personnel executive of each division has in his office a locked wall cabinet. Within the cabinet, which is unlocked only for authorized persons, is a divisional organization chart, displaying the results of its long-range executive manpower planning. To each position on the chart are attached three removable colored cards, each with a name and birth date: that of the present incumbent, his understudy, and another possible candidate. The colors indicate the current evaluation of each man's long-range potential. These mechanics reflect a simple but highly effective system of long-range executive manpower planning based on thorough, periodic, written performance appraisals by line superiors.

That much formality is rare in the executive manpower planning of even the most successful companies. In fact, I know of one outstanding company whose current plan is recorded on a single sheet of paper in the president's desk. But some form of executive manpower planning is essential in providing the right types and numbers of executives. And a simple form of planning that is *used* is far preferable to elaborate charts and colored diagrams that no one has time to bother with. Such elaborate systems are frequently no more than monuments to the eager efforts of a personnel executive motivated by a chief executive's lip service to "management development." Too often, companies approach executive manpower planning as an isolated and somewhat rarefied technique instead of a useful and integral part of an overall system of management.

Planning retirements is the easiest part of manpower planning because of the certainty that every executive must ultimately retire for reasons of age. If retirement is mandatory at 65 (now almost standard policy in U.S. large-scale enter-

prise) the time at which any executive is to be replaced can
be precisely determined. Whether promotion, resignation, ill-
health, or death may call for the replacement of a given executive in a given period is difficult if not impossible to predict;
but certain it is that nearly every executive will have to be
replaced one or more times in his career for one or more of
these reasons. Obviously this calls for added depth as insurance against these unpredictable certainties.

The chance of losing promising executive talent is increased by the rapid growth of executive recruiting or executive search firms. These firms provide an effective means for
filling positions from the outside, but the other side of the
equation is loss of talent by the supplying company. Thus, there
is need for added depth of talent—as well as attention to
executive motivation—as additional insurance against this new
source of executive loss.

The most successful companies plan for these uncertainties
by *requiring* every executive to develop and name an understudy. Such planned depth of talent provides a sound basis for
growth either through expansion or through acquisition. Many
an attractive acquisition is passed over by companies that lack
executive talent to staff the acquired business. Conversely,
many companies become available for acquisition simply for
lack of continuity of effective management. So the successful
company fosters its own growth by planning sufficient intake
and development of executive trainees to provide executive
talent in adequate depth.

The successful company that plans for ample (though not
excessive) depth of talent need not be concerned when an
occasional high-potential man leaves. Moreover, talent in depth
will stimulate company growth and thereby minimize such
losses. (You may recall my earlier reference to Armstrong

Cork's strategy of acquiring run-down businesses so their executive talent would have something to chew on.)

But developing an *over-supply* of executive talent—hoarding, so to speak—is not only expensive but a waste of a scarce national resource. Real talent is ambitious; and when it becomes clear that there *is* an over-supply, some of the most able executives will accept or even seek positions outside the company. In the long term, therefore, any over-supply is self-correcting.

Manpower planning should be done at the corporate level. In a divisionalized business, the individual development of high-potential executives should in part be programmed through interdivisional transfers. High-caliber executives are a resource of the total company. The over-all development of this resource should be the responsibility of a highly qualified and respected head of the corporate personnel administration department. It is done that way in the company with the locked wall cabinets.

Executive manpower planning, except for the intake of college and graduate school recruits, should be based on an organized program of performance evaluations (see Chapter 8). Given sensible performance evaluations, the techniques of executive manpower planning are simple enough; but the will to manage cannot be made fully effective unless this simple procedure becomes a real, actively used part of a company's system of management.

Recruitment and Selection

A company must compete not only for share-of-market but for share-of-talent. Since executive talent interested in a career in business is in limited supply throughout the free world, one important purpose of a company's management system and strategy should be to attract and select from that limited supply, retain the selected talent, and make it productive.

Because most successful companies promote from within, most recruiting of executive talent is done at colleges and (increasingly) at graduate schools. From time to time, however, every business needs to fill positions requiring experienced executive talent that is not available inside the company.

Competition for talent: For many years John W. Gardner —Secretary of Health, Education, and Welfare, former president of Carnegie Corporation, author of *Excellence* and *Self-Renewal,* and a keen observer and analyst of contemporary society—followed the practice of discussing one major topic in each annual report of Carnegie Corporation. In one year his topic was "The Great Talent Hunt," of which he wrote:

> We are witnessing a revolution in society's attitude toward men and women of high ability and advanced training. For the first time in history, such men and women are very much in demand on a very wide scale. Throughout the ages, human societies have always been extravagantly wasteful of talent. Today, as a result of far-reaching social and technological developments in our society, we are forced to search for talent and to use it effectively. Among the historic changes which have marked our era, this may in the long run prove to be one of the most profound. . . . Never in the history of America have so many people spent so much money in the search for talent.[3]

The *Wall Street Journal's* "Labor Letter" column of August 3, 1965, contained this item:

> *Banks Scramble to Fill Openings From Top to Bottom*
>
> The president of Chicago's Mid-City National complains of a "continual shortage of top-flight executives; we're constantly looking for good men." . . . An Eastern bank says it has doubled its recruiting outlays in the past two years. For

some banks, the gaps are fatal; many of the postwar mergers can be laid to shortages of capable executives, a New York banker says.

The world-wide growth in demand for executive talent in business is increasing with new technological advances and the growing complexities of operations that challenge every successful company. The demand for and development of manager talent were dealt with in detail in a remarkable statement by Lord Heyworth, then chairman of Unilever Limited, at the annual stockholders' meeting in London in 1956.[4] Lord Heyworth described Unilever as an Anglo-Dutch partnership operating several hundred companies in more than 40 different countries, with a total at that time of 270,000 employees, of whom 22,600 (or some 8 percent) were managers—16,400 first-line supervisors and 6,000 middle and senior managers.

He then went on to show that in the comparatively simple plantation operations in Nigeria and the Cameroons, managers made up only 3 percent of total employment. Managers accounted for 11 percent of total employment in the more complicated operations of the United Kingdom and Holland. In the United States, because of the "higher degree of mechanization and the more sophisticated environment," managers made up 15 percent of Unilever's total employment. Lord Heyworth concluded his analysis with this statement:

> . . . As the business expands we shall need more managers and, as I suggested earlier, the pattern which is unfolding is one in which the proportion of managers in relation to the whole will continue to rise, and this at a time when the competition to secure the services of managers is everywhere increasing. Therefore we can never let up.
>
> We must not expect the universities, schools, and technical

colleges to provide the answer unaided. We must continually examine our methods of recruitment and selection. We must take every opportunity to bring on and upgrade our own people from the lower levels. We must all of us understand the importance of training. For if we fail to do these things, and to do them in every country where Unilever is to be found, our failure will not be slow to show itself in the results which are laid before you.

Lord Heyworth's analysis of an increased proportion of managers with increasing technology and complexity squared with Du Pont's view. An article some years ago in the *Du Pont Stockholder* points out that more than 25 percent of Du Pont's employees at that time were classified as management personnel. Looking to the future, the article said:

> Great as the increase has been, business leadership today is now faced with the prospect of a pressing shortage of management personnel which may provide a serious impediment to future development. Over the next ten years, it is expected that a net increase of at least 50 percent will be required, in addition to replacing the normal losses from retirement, illness, change of occupation, and death.[5]

My observations indicate that these views of Lever and Du Pont have been borne out by subsequent experience, although this trend is currently being challenged by the influence of the computer. As business grows more complex, the computer permits simplification of decision making; and some evidence has accumulated that the computer has reduced the need for middle managers. How the influence of these countervailing forces on middle management will ultimately balance out is difficult to foresee. The normal resistance to change that exists in every enterprise will tend to delay resolution of this issue. It is clear, however, that the computer will reduce the number of people doing repetitive tasks, including lower level executive positions; and the net effect will undoubtedly be to increase the proportion of executive-type positions.[6]

There is no hard evidence and very little opinion, however, that the computer will reduce the demand for *high-talent* executives. In fact, the greater quantity and higher quality of information that the computer makes available require more rigorous analysis and permit greater creativity in decision making. Consequently executives may well find their jobs more intellectually demanding because the range of decision alternatives is greater.

Therefore, as the demand for high-talent executives increases during the next decade, the need for developing a strategic approach to executive manpower development and deployment becomes more important. In fact, executive manpower strategy should rank just as high as user and profit strategy.

Unfortunately, business's growing need for high-talent executives has not been matched by an increase in the supply of raw material. Business educators are concerned because such a small proportion of the country's outstanding brainpower is being attracted to business careers. Speaking on "The Role of the Business School in the Economic Development of the Country," George P. Baker, Dean of Harvard Business School, said:

> No adequate statistics are available to indicate precisely what portion of the top 10 percent of each college graduating class chooses business as a career. The best estimates we have been able to uncover to date, however, indicate that no more than about 7 percent go on to graduate study in business administration, compared with up to 20 percent going on to law school and 22 percent to medical school. If business is to meet

successfully the challenges outlined today, if we believe that the activities and decisions of managers at all levels of economic organizations generate or respond to the forces conducive to growth, then it is our responsibility to find ways to attract more of the brightest young people into our schools of business.

Business executives generally have both a long-term opportunity and a responsibility to the nation to help make business a more attractive career for the country's outstanding brainpower. If they take this responsibility seriously, the individual company will benefit in the process from the increased productivity of its own executives. Meantime, however, the individual company should plan its strategy and gear its operations generally to meet severe competition in the market for high-caliber manpower.

Improving campus recruiting performance: One way to meet increasing competition for talent is, of course, through more effective recruiting at colleges and graduate schools. Discussions with university placement officials and with students themselves convince me that both the quantity and the quality of corporate recruiting effort can be improved. It is surprising how poorly even leading companies do on the campus.

I believe that the single greatest determinant of the productivity of campus recruiting is *feedback to the campus.* How current graduates view the company will be very heavily influenced by what they hear about it from prior graduates. The high-talent graduate can easily find out from them about how the company is managed, how attractive the opportunities for advancement appear to be, and how the new man is handled during his first couple of years. Compared with this kind of feedback, even the most beguiling recruiters and the most astute recruiting activities can only marginally affect the campus evaluation of a company—and its success in recruiting high-talent graduates.

Improving the way the company is managed and its growth and profit outlook is really the best way to step up campus recruiting of high-talent people—and this, of course, is a long-term purpose of the programmed management system. Thus the successful company has the best chance to recruit the largest number of outstanding men from colleges and graduate schools. The companies that need talent the least can get it most easily, and vice versa. So the best answer to improved recruiting performance lies in improved management.

Over the short term, however, most companies can get an attractive pay-off by improving the way they treat high-talent campus recruits during their first couple of years. The president of a very large corporation once complained to me about the small number of men his company was able to attract from graduate business schools. I asked him how they were treated. "We put them right into our two-year training squad for our college trainees," he replied. "We give them no special breaks. We're not going to have any crown princes in our company." He was avoiding the "crown prince" problem with graduate school men, all right—by attracting so few of them.

Career discussions over the years with several hundred graduate business school men have convinced me that this is the way the outstanding ones want to be treated in their first two years:

1. They want work that is challenging and important. They do not want routine work requiring little brainpower, and they resent menial tasks designed to teach them humility or bring them to heel.

2. Outstanding men want responsibility just as soon as they are ready for it, and they expect an early chance to show

whether they *are* ready. They do not want youth to count against them in getting that chance. In my high-talent survey two out of three who returned questionnaires said that men should be given real job responsibility more quickly.

3. Outstanding men want their ideas and suggestions taken seriously. They do not want to be brushed off or told not to rock the boat. They do *not* expect all their suggestions to be adopted. But when they are turned down they expect to be told the reasons.

4. Outstanding men do not expect to be treated tenderly or given special favors. They want to be judged rigorously on merit—and recognized accordingly.

In my opinion, the competition for business talent is so keen that the successful company must find ways of giving outstanding graduates what they want. Unfortunately, too many top-management executives are too much guided by their own career experience. Most of them, who came into business when the competition for talent was less severe, just aren't facing the facts of competition in the present-day talent market. Fortunately, the things that outstanding graduates want are, in my opinion, good for the company; and by giving them what they want, management will also be making better use of a scarce and valuable national resource.

The answer lies, I believe, in developing company strategy, philosophy, policies, and programs that are more specifically geared to the attitudes and ambitions of the high-talent man.

Here are a few do's and don'ts for improving results from the campus recruiting effort:

1. Don't over-sell the company or the opportunities it offers. In my high-talent survey, some 20 percent of those who replied said their firms could improve recruiting and selection if they would "stop over-selling the company." High-talent men are

sophisticated enough to appreciate that there are negatives as well as positives in every company situation. They want the employer to level with them. And they'll learn the negatives, anyway, just as soon as they join the company.

2. Don't use a "wining and dining" approach. Because of the tight market, especially at the graduate school level, the better candidates may have as many as a dozen offers, and it is tempting to try to influence them through entertainment. But this approach usually backfires.

3. Do some of your recruiting with outstanding recent graduates now on your payroll—men who have made rapid progress and hence are good representatives. This will provide a good feedback and give the current graduate a chance to see himself through the eyes of someone not too high up the executive ladder. Enthusiasm from these recent graduates is usually more convincing than the company "party line" coming from a professional recruiting executive.

4. Base campus and graduate school selection decisions— like other selection decisions—chiefly on the individual's basic qualities. These can best be determined by examining his prior performance in college and high school activities, summer work experience, even Boy Scout and other junior activities. An early and continuing pattern of superior performance is the best assurance of future success.

Recruiting for higher-level positions: Even though a company does an outstanding campus recruiting job and promotes from within whenever possible, high-level positions must occasionally be filled from the outside.

In such cases, the first step is to determine specifically the basic personal qualifications needed to fill the position successfully: analytical skill, imagination, administrative ability, leadership, etc. Too many positions are filled from the outside chiefly on the basis of work in the same industry or in the same type of job. My observations convince me that, even in high-level positions, basic personal qualities are more important than prior experience in the same industry or type of work. Job approach and the requirements for personal success are better determinants of future success than the technical content of the job.

Even managers who believe strongly in promotion from within often fail to really search the company for someone with enough basic qualities for the job to deserve a chance at it. Although I can't prove it, I believe that the insider who seems 65 percent qualified for the job is likely to outperform the typical outsider who seems 90 percent qualified. Such assessments are apt to be unbalanced, because the weaknesses of the insider are known, while those of the outsider are hard to learn accurately in advance. Since an insider's success will improve the morale and productivity of the executive group generally, it is usually worth taking a substantial risk on an insider, particularly if the only count against him is youth or lack of experience for the job.

Recruiting or placement specialists provide the best-organized means of finding candidates for positions that cannot be filled from within. Although a competent recruiter will screen candidates, it is important that company executives not only make the selection, but recognize that the choice is actually their own responsibility. If they regard the new man as the recruiter's selection, subconsciously they will feel less responsible for helping the outsider succeed once he is on the job.

Making reliable reference checks on the competence of the experienced outsider requires special diligence and resourcefulness. Complete and objective evaluations are generally hard to get. People want to be helpful to the man who is out of a job; and they generally don't want to lose the man who is still with the company. Moreover, a friend, former employer, or current associate of the job candidate has little incentive to be completely forthright with a stranger. Consequently, checking should preferably be done in person or by telephone.

Some checks should be made by a person who has not interviewed the candidate and hence will not subconsciously seek to justify his own evaluation. In trying to get an objective evaluation, the inquirer should emphasize to the reference that the candidate will only be harmed if he gets into a job he cannot perform. Checks should be made with people whose names have not been supplied by the candidate. And a definite effort should be made to identify the individual's weaknesses.

Even the best techniques of defining qualifications and interviewing and checking candidates for higher-level positions cannot eliminate all mistakes in selection. One wise chief executive I know rates the chances of an outsider's success no better than 50-50. By providing enough college and graduate-school executive candidates within the organization, however, the need to bring in outsiders can be held to a minimum.

Developing Executives

Management fashions, like women's fashions, have their fads. One management fad of the past decade has been management development. Enormous numbers of words and dollars have been lavished on this activity. My observations convince me that, apart from alerting managers more fully to the need for management development, these expenditures have not been very productive.

For example, I asked the vice president for personnel administration of a machinery company how the company developed its executives. He handed me a four-page typewritten memorandum, saying, "Here are some of the things that we try to get our executives to learn for themselves and teach their subordinates." I found that the memorandum, which was headed "Executive Techniques," was a list of 68 do's and don't's, such as: Be considerate, be consistent, do not grumble, do not rationalize, be a good listener.

If that seems inane, consider the contents of a course bought by another company to train its executives. It is entitled "How To Be a Good Executive," and contains "100 specific points." Many of these 100 points have from 10 to 25 subpoints. Here is one of 17 subpoints under Main Point 99: "You do not let personal feelings, preferences, and prejudices influence your actions in your work."

Probably more platitudes have been written about how to be an executive than about any other phase of management. These recipes do no harm. If studied by the man who really *wants* to be an executive, most of them will be helpful. My purpose is not to pile up further platitudes, but rather to show how executive development is done in the most success- ful companies and put it in perspective as part of a system of management. In fact, I believe that only when executive de- velopment *is* part of a system of management will it be really successful.

I have observed that in successful companies the way the business is managed is what chiefly determines whether execu- tives develop and whether they want to learn. Since the best executive development is *self*-development, a real desire to learn is essential.

Self-development of any kind is stimulated most strongly by the pressure of a real, live situation that demands performance. Note that the demand for performance comes from the situation, not just the boss. Consider the young, inexperienced men who in wartime successfully commanded troops, ships, submarines, and airplanes. Their own lives and the lives of others depended on their success. Again, consider how quickly Egyptian ship pilots successfully replaced foreign pilots when Nasser nationalized the Suez Canal in 1956. World opinion held that the task of piloting a ship through the narrow, shallow 103-mile canal was so complicated that Nasser could not keep the canal operating. But a week after 140 foreign pilots had quit their jobs, Associated Press reported, a small corps of Egyptian pilots had safely guided 253 ships through the canal.[7]

The situation that demands executive performance in business is a job where the man feels the full weight of responsibility. His development flourishes because the situation demands *self*-development. Because the total work situation is a learning situation, development comes naturally and virtually automatically. As John Gardner says in *Self-Renewal:* "The development of abilities is at least in part a dialogue between the individual and his environment. If he has it to give and the environment demands it, the ability will develop." [8]

What, then, are the characteristics of a management system that creates the situation which provides the greatest stimulus for executives to develop themselves? There is probably no business executive who works harder or more effectively than the successful individual proprietor of his own business in a free-enterprise economy. He works with zest and determination. He has no one to train him. His effectiveness derives chiefly from two basic elements of his situation: (1) he is responsible and (2) he is accountable. In short, he succeeds or fails—in terms of money, pride, and work satisfaction—in direct ratio to what he accomplishes in his work. The payoff comes in accomplishment, not in effort.

Thus, the challenge to large-scale enterprise is to create the work situation that puts every executive on his own as much as possible. The most successful companies achieve this by making every executive responsible and accountable for his own decisions and actions. These two terms are not synonymous. An executive is "responsible" when he has a clearly defined job and is generally expected to carry out the assigned duties. He is "accountable" when he also has the authority needed to carry out his responsibilities, and the certainty that he will be judged by his own performance and rewarded or penalized accordingly. Thus, responsibility is determined chiefly by the plan of organization. Accountability, however, is determined chiefly by the actions and attitudes of superiors in dealing with their subordinates. These, in turn, are governed by company philosophy and other components of the management system.

In establishing both the responsibility and accountability of an executive, the first essential is delegation. Beyond that, the principal aids to self-development on the job are performance evaluation and coaching by superiors. In discussing only these three developmental ingredients, I'll assume the existence of a wholesome working atmosphere (see Chapter 8). And I'll omit any discussion of outside courses, conferences, internal formal training programs, and other worthwhile but supplementary aids.

Delegation: Here is an excellent discussion of delegation and executive development from Lord Heyworth's statement cited above:

> But when all is said and done, when we have made the fullest use of courses, secondments, conferences, study panels and other extraneous aids of this kind, we come back to my starting-point, that fundamentally the training of the senior

manager, as of the junior, is done on the job. And a man can-not develop his full qualities in his job unless those above him give him scope to do so. This means that we must truly prac-tice delegation, not just pay lip-service to the principle.

Delegation does not mean just sitting back with your feet up and leaving a subordinate to do the work; it should be a positive act of trust. It does not, I think, come naturally to most people. We are all inclined to give a man a job to do and then to look over his shoulder to make sure that he is not making a mistake. This is a tendency which must be resisted, as must the inclination to delegate only to those whom we regard as men who will play safe. This is no way to create a forward-looking and progressive body of managers.

Management cannot be lively and efficient unless there is true delegation. Conversely, people will be unwilling to dele-gate unless management is lively and efficient. If these two propositions look like creating a vicious circle anywhere in the business, we must break through it.

The "vicious circle" to which Lord Heyworth referred is merely a further instance of the systemic or reciprocating operation of the various managing processes. Since a success-ful business needs high-caliber executive talent, and since only a successful business can attract such talent, the company's strategy, policies, and programs should be designed accord-ingly.

As we saw in Chapter 5, delegation should begin with a clear definition of responsibility and authority. An ambitious man will reach for responsibility, and company philosophy should encourage him to do so. But a good team player will also be reluctant to encroach on the responsibilities of others.

In fact, delegation will be facilitated if company practice treats positions as *offices* occupied by particular incumbents, instead of permitting each person to carve out the scope of his own job and establish his own authority. This *office* concept, as we have seen, is facilitated by the growing practice of spelling out authority in written position descriptions.

Delegation is impeded in a company that emphasizes personal standing rather than positions. In such a company, each executive must think first of his personal standing instead of his responsibilities and the facts on which his decisions and actions should be based. Conversely, delegation is easier in a company that takes a fact-founded approach to decisions and actions. In such an organization, executives at all levels look at the facts together instead of watching one another's political gains and losses.

Either giving too-detailed instructions in advance or making a too-detailed review after action has been taken results in poor delegation. Any subordinate already has certain automatic performance guides: policies, plans, and budgets. If, in addition, his superior tells him step by step how to take action, the subordinate feels too much like a puppet. His freedom to think for and learn by himself is limited, and his opportunity to learn through mistakes is denied. The results are virtually the same when the subordinate knows his actions will be subject to detailed review: instead of using his own judgment, he will then try to learn or guess what the superior would do.

During his term as Secretary of Defense, Charles E. Wilson, ex-president of GM, was asked whether he had given detailed orders to the Secretary of the Army. Mr. Wilson replied: "You never give anyone orders to such a degree; that isn't the way it is done. I mean it's like trying to tell someone how to suck eggs. You give him a job and let him go and suck it his way."

Delegation is impaired by top-management executives who expect their subordinates to have detailed operating information in mind. Here is a typical complaint: "I cringe whenever I hear the president wants to see me. I know he is going to ask me things about my operations that I don't know. He doesn't discuss plans and results—just operating details that are so inconsequential that I don't know them or *want* to know them. But I try to keep informed on minutiae so he won't think I'm stupid. As a matter of fact, I waste so much time and get into so many details with my subordinates that they must think I don't have confidence in them. So the disease spreads down the line."

Many otherwise able chief executives have the strange belief that asking high-level managers questions about details will "keep them on their toes." Actually, it keeps them back on their heels. Certainly the practice does nothing to develop them or the managers below them, each of whom must keep his superior informed.

When relatively minor matters for decision tend to float upward, delegation is almost certainly incomplete or ineffectual. This upward float takes place for a combination of reasons: subordinates do not know whether they have authority; they want to avoid criticism by playing it safe; and the superior, by showing he is *willing* to decide, makes it easy for subordinates to *let* him decide. The upward float is human, and only the superior can prevent it.

In summary, superiors with the best records of developing managers (1) use fact-founded and objective methods of dealing with their subordinates, (2) avoid detailed instructions and review, (3) don't make on-the-spot requests for detailed operating information, (4) require their subordinates to decide, and (5) permit subordinates to make a reasonable number of errors.

Performance evaluation: I recall a high-level executive whose poor performance was widely but covertly discussed throughout his company. Asking another executive how this person had been selected for the job, I learned that he had been chosen after coming to the president's attention during a divisional meeting. This is not an isolated example. Selection on the basis of "visibility" is common. In a company that lacks an organized program for evaluating performance as a basis for executive compensation and advancement, it is excusable and even, to a degree, necessary.

A policy of compensating and advancing executives on the basis of performance needs to be backed by a procedure and program for making and using written evaluations. And organized performance evaluation can also be a useful tool in developing executive competence.

Many companies, however, go through all the work of evaluating people without getting full benefit from the program—chiefly because they do not really believe in its value. Filling out evaluation forms and then not making effective use of the results is a costly and frustrating exercise. In fact, form without substance always reduces profits, because costs are incurred without producing useful results.

Du Pont has demonstrated the value of a well-organized and tightly administered evaluation program in making decisions about people and helping them improve their performance. Observation of the profit-making value of such programs prompts the following comments and suggestions:

1. A performance evaluation program, together with the necessary procedures and forms, should be tailor-made by every company for its own particular purposes—not copied from anyone else. There is no accepted standard of what is right in all circumstances. Of course the successful experiences of others can be useful, but they must always be adapted to the company's own circumstances—"what really works for us."

2. Performance evaluation can be properly done only if a written report is filled out at regular intervals. Written re-

ports are necessary to be sure that performance elements and standards are not overlooked by the evaluator, and that he is required to think through and put down correct information in a responsible fashion.

Preventing the unfair practice of basing compensation and advancement decisions chiefly on recent performance requires a series of reports. Performance that is fresh in memory is not necessarily representative, and it cannot give a picture free of the distortions of recent enthusiasms or disappointments.

3. When performance evaluations are made but not used, the whole program soon dies on the vine. Executives must be convinced that evaluations actually affect compensation and advancement decisions and the development of people. Otherwise, they will give up making and recording evaluations—or will just go through the cost-producing motions. Consequently, in making their decisions, top-management executives need to make real and visible use of evaluation forms.

Coaching: A 38-year-old sales executive once told me he had never received any real training until he had been transferred to his current territory. "In my last territory," he said, "I got good experience but no training. My regional manager wanted the men to like him, so he never told us anything unpleasant and never gave us a real working-over. My present boss is a different sort of guy. He really tells me how I'm doing, especially what I've done wrong and how I can improve. I don't like him as well as my last boss, but I respect him more—and I'm learning more. I only wish I'd had him for a boss five years sooner."

From many such discussions I've learned that the superior who really levels with his subordinates about how they are doing and how they can improve usually wins their admiration, their respect, and even their affection. By leveling with his

men, he is doing his developmental job; and he will get satisfaction from seeing them grow in competence.

I recall once interviewing an executive with whom I had
first talked five years before. In the interval he had had two
advancements, and his growth in executive competence and
zest for his job were so impressive that I asked him what had
caused the change. He explained that his last two superiors
had both delegated full responsibility and leveled with him
about his mistakes. The value of the results, both to the business and to the man himself, was pleasantly obvious.

Three comments made on replies to my high-talent survey
reinforce these points.

> "Your boss is your best teacher. Some supplemental training
> may be desirable, but doing is the best schooling."

> "I believe that development for young men comes most
> quickly by giving them great opportunity to perform and by
> ensuring that they have the 'ear' of a mature senior man for
> counsel. In short, let the energy and aggressiveness of youth
> be coupled with the mature judgment of a senior officer."

> "Frequently review his shortcomings and what more is
> expected of him. Above all, be frank."

My discussions with executives over the years have led me
to some definite conclusions about coaching:

1. Too often the superior is reluctant to level with a subordinate about his faults and weaknesses from fear of hurting
his feelings, or at any rate, of plunging into "awkward" or
"difficult" discussions. If such executives only realized how
hungry most subordinates are for real criticism, they would
take the plunge—and would find the discussions much easier
and more rewarding than they had anticipated.

2. Coaching should be given promptly, while the facts

about performance are fresh in the minds of both subordinate and superior. Delay diminishes the value of coaching.

3. As part of an organized program, the coach should use the written performance report as a tool. This will make it clear to the subordinate *how* he is being evaluated. It will also give him the benefit of specific suggestions on how to overcome recorded weaknesses.

4. Superiors should try to translate specific praise and criticisms into guidelines that will be applicable in other situations. This can be done by relating the comments to some objective, strategy, principle, policy, or procedure. Every executive or supervisor should recognize that if he is to perform well, he must be an on-the-job teacher. And he should unabashedly act like one.

In General Motors, Armstrong Cork, and other well-managed businesses, development of subordinates is one test of good performance. "If I got hit by a bus this afternoon," said John Blamy, manufacturing manager of GM's Pontiac division, "there'd be at least four men right here—I mean within the manufacturing group at Pontiac—ready to take my place tomorrow morning. If we had to look elsewhere, even within Pontiac, I'd have shirked my responsibility." [9]

Job rotation: Planned job rotation is the way to the top at Du Pont. General Foods makes frequent transfers between divisions. Federated Stores moves men from store to store. Texaco shifts marketing men from one part of the country to another. "If I were telling my boy how to get ahead at General Motors," said Elliot M. Estes, then general manager of the Pontiac division, "I would emphasize hard work and a willingness to switch jobs."

Work in staff jobs trains a man to think, to analyze, to be creative. A tour of duty by a division executive in corporate staff work will make him more effective when he returns to his division. Meanwhile, the corporate staff activity will have benefited from his operating viewpoint.

Job rotation is a proven developer of executive ability, but even those who believe in the principle are often reluctant to apply it. Youth, lack of experience, and risk of failure are typical rationales for not making a job rotation decision. But they are not good excuses.

The way to do it is just to do it: Assume the risks and the costs, in the knowledge that it works well most of the time. Successful company-wide planning of rotations is done that way. John Gardner says in *Self-Renewal:*

> In an organization, a well-designed system of personnel rotation will yield high dividends not only in the growth of the individual but in organizational fluidity. Free movement of personnel throughout the organization reduces barriers to internal communication, diminishes hostility between divisions and ensures a freer flow of information and ideas.[10]

Simplicity of development: Like so many other aspects of managing a business, developing executives is simple but not easy. A man must feel the full weight of real responsibility. This requires full delegation of authority and the knowledge that he will be held accountable for results. He needs to know where he stands and how he is doing. He needs to shift from job to job. And he needs and wants to be leveled with so he knows how to improve his performance. When these simple things are done effectively and consistently in the atmosphere of a well-managed business, they will develop the greatest resource a company can have: competent executive manpower.

Advancement and Separation

The possibility of advancement is, of course, an important, if not the most important, incentive for improved executive performance and development in business. Advancement not only means increased compensation, prestige, and power, but carries with it the challenge of more responsibility.

Not surprisingly, nearly 70 percent of those in my high-talent survey who had stayed with their companies gave "good opportunities for advancement" as a reason. Almost as many of those who had changed their jobs said they had sought—among other things—a better chance for advancement. Here are some of their typical comments about previous employers:

> "No personnel development. Management not interested in going ahead, just wanted to keep what they had."

> "There was little freedom to transfer within the organization to a higher position in another section. Advancement is a matter of attrition."

> "The company was badly over-staffed. Just too many good men waiting in line."

In any kind of organization, advancement is an important tool of executive personnel administration. Commenting on the advancement of Nicholas Katzenbach to Attorney General after four years of good work in the Department of Justice, *The New York Times* said editorially:

> One important way of attracting public servants of conspicuous quality is to reward disinterested service. Talent begets talent because good men like to work in an atmosphere where they know the man at the top recognizes superior performance when he sees it. In promoting Mr. Katzenbach, the President demonstrates that he believes in this principle and is willing to act on it.[11]

Since responsibility is the great developer of executive competence, the best-managed businesses advance men early in their careers—in Du Pont and IBM, for example. Most well-managed companies find early advancement is a good way to attract and hold high-caliber men, as well as to develop executive ability, but as one man in my high-talent survey commented: "Get rid of the idea that the well-qualified individual must be with the company 20 years before he can be broadened." An early advancement policy makes such good campus feedback that some companies even advertise it in college and graduate school publications.

Not all advancements prove successful, of course. Even when the man advanced has plenty of age, tenure, and experience, he may fail to perform effectively in the new job after a fair opportunity to demonstrate his competence. When this happens, the company faces one of the thorniest questions in business: to separate or not to separate.

Sound motivation requires penalties as well as rewards. Whether or not advancement represents the extreme reward, separation clearly represents the extreme penalty. Every manager is reluctant to apply penalties, especially the extreme penalty of removing a man from his job or asking him to resign.

One hallmark of outstanding management, however, is willingness to face up promptly to problems—including problems of poor performance that may involve separation. To keep a poor performer in the job after a reasonable trial period is unfair to the company, to other executives, and usually to the man himself. Condoning poor performance has adverse repercussions throughout the entire management system; conversely, the willingness by top management to face the facts and make dismissals fairly has a multiplier effect in building respect for top management and for the management system.

In one very successful company I know, an effort is made to move the poor performer back to the level in which he had performed successfully before he was advanced—preferably not to the same job but to a comparable one in different circumstances. In fact, experience in a number of companies with which I am familiar refutes the common assumption that a man cannot be successfully demoted: It all depends on the man, the circumstances, and the way the demotion is handled.

But when demotion or transfer to another job in the company is not feasible, it is better to separate the poor performer than to let him stay in the job. It should, of course, be understood that advancement always carries with it the risk of removal and even dismissal. Great universities and great professional firms have "up-or-out" policies—which are accepted as a condition of employment—requiring continuing achievement within specified periods or by specified ages.

It is surprising how often a man dismissed from one company will perform well in another. Perhaps he is stimulated to put out more or perhaps it is just that different circumstances permit him to use his abilities better. Although I can think of tragic dismissal cases, I can also think of many men who have profited personally from dismissals, going on to better jobs or opportunities elsewhere. One advantage of early advancement is that it provides testing at an early age. If a man fails the test and must be dismissed, he is still young enough to get a job that uses his full potential effectively.

No matter how agonizing separation decisions may be, company success sometimes requires that they be made. No company can increase its volume and share-of-market, improve its return on investment, or provide for continuity of effective management if it is burdened with poor performers at any executive level. The ultimate test of the will to manage is the will to dismiss.

Executive Compensation

The use of financial incentives to improve executive performance and encourage executive development is a broad and complex subject. Bonus and stock-option plans have powerfully stimulated executive performance throughout American business, and they might well be more broadly used in Europe. Without treating executive compensation in depth, I feel that three observations on this important tool of executive personnel administration are in order here:

First, I don't believe money motivates executives as strongly as is generally thought. I *don't* mean by this to deny that executives work for money; obviously, they do want and expect to be well paid for good performance. The negative incentive of a steeply progressive individual income tax—and its devastating effects on the economy—is all that is needed to show that money is an important incentive. I simply mean that non-monetary incentives are more important than they are generally thought to be. Or, to put it another way: No company should rely too heavily on money to attract executives, hold them, and make them productive. It takes more than money to build the primary resource of a business.

Let me illustrate that assertion:

■ More than one executive has told me in confidence of turning down a job offering substantially higher rewards in terms of stock options or after-tax cash compensation, because the financial differential was canceled out by attractive nonfinancial factors in his present company and/or unattractive nonfinancial factors in the other company.

■ Executives frequently accept positions in other companies at comparable or even lower compensation because of other favorable factors such as advancement opportunities, work challenge, or working climate.

■ It is common for highly compensated executives to admit, in confidence, that they are working well below capacity because of lack of opportunity, inadequate work challenge, or a poor working climate.

Yes, money is important. But it takes much more than money to attract and retain a high-caliber man. Especially does it take more than high pay to make such a man work at the top of his capacity. And the higher his tax bracket, of course, the less effective money is as an incentive and the more nonfinancial incentives must be relied on.

Second, the complex mechanics of administering executive compensation frequently impair the over-all effectiveness of executive personnel administration in large companies. In such organizations, organized salary administration based on job evaluation is essential for paying people equitably. But elaborate point systems and other inflexibilities can handicap rather than aid good executive personnel administration. In one large company, for example, a point system, combined with a policy of providing similar titles in all divisions, so distorts the salary scale as to inhibit interdivisional transfers. In many companies delays in reevaluating jobs prevent advancements and transfers that would help develop executives and improve company performance.

Third, a company whose philosophy calls for fairness and equity in everything it does will reap a big payoff in administering executive compensation. Executives recognize the difficulties of administering compensation fairly. They know that instant equity may not be possible when executives are brought in from the outside. But if the company philosophy gives them confidence that fairness and equity will be achieved as rapidly as feasible, they will not be troubled by minor, temporary inequities in compensation.

In a 1965 message to Congress, President Johnson said:

> The success of all our [defense] policies depends upon our ability to attract, develop fully, utilize, and retain the talents of outstanding men and women in the military services.

Certainly the same is true in a company. But retaining the talents of outstanding people is not enough—they must be made productive through development, incentives, discipline, and leadership. Programmed management is concerned with all these elements, their interaction, and their mutual relations with every other element in the system.

7

Operational Planning and Control: The Track and the Signals

Every year for five years a consumer products division of a large diversified corporation had budgeted and achieved an increase in volume and profits. Based on those operating results, major capital expenditures were made for new plant facilities. Then, within months, the division's healthy profits turned to sickening loss. The chief executive was stunned. How could it have happened?

The explanation was simple. Each year the division had expanded its well-established brand into a new geographic area. In doing so, it had cut back on advertising and promotion in its established territories and channeled the money into the new ones. For five years the added volume and profit from the new territories covered up the division's static or declining market shares in the old. But then stiffening competition put a stop to the division's territorial expansion and obliged it to step up advertising and promotional expenditures everywhere. Inevitably, profits melted away.

The chief executive first dealt with that crisis by closing down plants and drastically cutting costs. Then he set in motion a corporation-wide overhaul of operational planning and control. Like other chief executives, he had learned that unless these two components are properly designed and work well the management system cannot be effective.

Planning: The Final Phases

The planning process, as we saw in Chapter 3, is a continuum, or spectrum. Its stages cannot be sharply divided in practice. Thus, strategic plans need to be carried through the final phases of the planning process. Otherwise top management, while exercising *financial* control through the budget, may be deprived of effective *operating* control. That is what the stunned chief executive paid a high price to learn.

The final phases of the planning process, described in this chapter, require executives at all levels to think deeply, at least once a year, about the destiny of each separate business and the company as a whole. Without this discipline, they are less likely to identify major problems to be dealt with and major opportunities to be seized. Moreover, these steps will force a review of strategic plans—or stimulate the inauguration of strategic planning if it has not already been done.

Therefore, with the full structure of the management system before us, it is now time to take up the final phases of the planning process: management programming, which is intermediate in time range, and the development of operational or short-range plans, on which the annual operating budget and capital budget are based. Finally, we look briefly at the control component of the management system, including ways that the management program and operational plan are used for control purposes. Thus the management program, the annual operating plan, and the budgets provide a track on which each business runs; and the controls flash signals to show how well the business is running.

I have deferred discussion of the operational end of the planning spectrum until now because the operating plan reflects the combined results and influences of all the other system components. Company philosophy, strategic plans, the management program, policies, organization plans, standards, and procedures are all wrapped up and brought into focus in the operating plan, which is designed to guide everyone's decisions and actions in the year ahead. In a sense, therefore, the operating plan both assembles the interdependent components of the management system and transmits their interactions within the system. To assure that user, profit, and manpower strategy will be fully effective in day-to-day operations, operational plans must be developed to carry out strategic plans and the management program in accordance with the total management system.

Benefits of Formal Planning

Formalized planning of the type described here and in Chapter 3 takes substantial executive time and effort to establish and perfect. Before deciding to embark on such a program, therefore, any management will want to be sure that it offers an attractive payoff. Here are the principal benefits that it can be counted on to provide:

■ *Information for improved top-management direction.* In any company—particularly a divisionalized one—the proposed planning program provides top management with better information for strategic planning and general direction. It assures a searching, factual, systematic analysis of each business at least once a year. This information enables top management to judge the relative attractiveness of each business and hence make better decisions in allocating capital and manpower resources among them. In addition, it brings to the surface for evaluation any product/market, competitive, and technological changes that might alter the outlook for any business.

■ *A common framework for top-management review.* Given a standard framework and systematic approach for challenging the forecasts and plans for each business or division, the higher executives in a diversified business are not required to know each business well in order to make a meaningful review of plans and budgets. Hence this kind of planning is particularly helpful in large-scale enterprises with many divisions engaged in different businesses.

■ *A focus on critical long-term profit factors.* This approach focuses top-management attention on key problems that may affect profits adversely and on opportunities that might be seized to increase profits. It requires the development of programs to meet goals, cope with problems, and seize opportunities. It ensures disciplined attention to divisional and corporate objectives and goals and their achievement.

■ *Control in advance.* Management programs and operational plans provide forward control. In a divisionalized business, for example, corporate management can—without appearing to "interfere"—systematically challenge the division's goals and programs before approving its operating plans and the related budget. The consumer products division that suffered an unexpected sharp drop in profits had a formal budgeting program. Its planning process, however, was rudimentary; top management routinely approved projected results without an opportunity to review and challenge the plans on which they were based.

■ *Delegation without abdication.* Soundly developed management programs assure top management of qualitative as well as quantitative assessments of all important elements of the business. Consequently, the chief executive can delegate with confidence, and still not abdicate his responsibilities. Thus this approach—with its emphasis on qualitative as well as financial results—is not in conflict with decentralization of authority to an autonomous division. But it does recognize the folly of giving a division manager complete responsibility for his activities, subject only to presenting financial plans that meet corporate objectives and goals.

Take the case of a very large corporation with more than a dozen divisions. Its chief executive boasted that he had carried decentralization to the point where headquarters people numbered fewer than 200, including general accounting personnel, his secretary, and his chauffeur. He had a well-developed budgeting program but no effective planning program. In fact, he had abdicated as well as delegated. He first lost control—and then lost his job.

Prior review of properly developed management programs and operational plans exposes both weaknesses and strengths so they can be dealt with in advance. This process would, for example, have identified in advance the potential sharp drop in profits that hit the consumer products division, and its story would have been a very different one. The unwise plant expenditures would have been avoided and other plans would have been made. Hence top management and any intermediate management should be required by the planning program to look behind the financial figures at least once a year and assure themselves of the soundness and long-term health and vitality of each of the company's businesses. Only then will delegation not also constitute abdication.

■ *Improved performance measurement.* Too many companies merely measure performance against planned *financial* results—usually as expressed in a budget. This approach is inadequate for good quantitative measurement and provides no qualitative measurement at all. As we have seen, a division or company can meet its budget and still not be under the effective control of top management. After years of satisfactory operating results, it can suddenly surprise top management with poor performance.

In contrast, a sound planning program provides top management with adequate bench marks, both quantitative and qualitative, for assessing projected performance. In fact, one new qualitative measure is provided through a determination of how well division and company executives carry out the planning process itself. Then during the year top management can assess actual performance by determining whether programs are being completed on time and whether planned results are being achieved, i.e., control against plan.

Thus an approved operational plan provides a much broader basis for top-management evaluation of division management performance than does an approved operating budget. Moreover, it permits each division manager, in turn, to judge the performance of his subordinates in much the same way. For example, it enables him to determine whether each key executive actually carries out his programs on time and achieves planned results.

Because of these solid benefits, managements that perfect this approach to planning become enthusiastic advocates of it. Underlying their enthusiasm, perhaps, are two important by-products of this type of planning. First, as a mechanism for setting priorities and coordinating activities, it helps executives at all levels concentrate their time and effort on the strategic fundamentals that govern long-term corporate success. Second, it serves as an excellent training device for executives at all levels, because they are all required to think deeply, creatively, and systematically about the company as a whole and each business that makes it up.

Makeup of the Management Program

The semifinal phase of this approach to planning calls for a written *management program* designed to convert broad strategic plans into specific intermediate-range implementing programs that can, in turn, be converted into the annual operating plan on which the budget is based.

Some planning programs move directly from the strategic plan to the operating plan. For example, the article discussing the Celanese planning program says:

> An operational plan puts flesh and sinew onto the strategic skeleton. If a strategic plan poses a challenging What, an operational plan answers with a convincing How, Who and When. Similarly, the goals of an operational plan are more concerned with expansion than with exploration, growth rather than change in direction.[1]

If it can be fitted in procedurally, however, I believe it is preferable to divide the planning spectrum into three phases and develop a separate management program. As mentioned earlier, the intermediate-range management program with its supporting data helps to test existing objectives and longer-range strategy and to force the development of any new strategic plans that may be needed. Moreover, the management program is tied deeply into the strategic plan and draws extensively on the analyses underlying it. Thus the management program is the core of the planning process, shading off from the strategic plan and into the operating plan. In fact, the planning procedure may well call for developing the management program and the operational plan almost simultaneously.

Like the strategic plan, but unlike the operating plan, the management program is not tied to any particular time period. The plans composing it will extend as far ahead as qualitative and quantitative projections can realistically be made—typically not less than two years nor more than six. Beyond that, in most businesses, unforeseeable changes will render the program pretty academic. On the other hand, in businesses such as chemicals and steel, new facilities have to be planned and constructed several years in advance. The test, then, is twofold: the *necessity* for forward planning and the *realism* of it. Of course, in projecting the business ahead for two to six years, there will be many plans that can be carried out almost immediately. Such plans will simply be included in the operational plan for the year ahead.

Thus it becomes the task of operational planning to convert the management program into the annual operating plan, i.e., to decide what part of the management program is to be carried out during the next budget year, and how. Hence, work scheduling is part of the operational plan, not of the management program.

Some managements may want to divide the planning spectrum in another way. As long as all the key elements of the planning process are included, the way it is divided doesn't really matter. If there are three phases, however, most of the specifics will be developed in preparing the management program and then refined in preparing the operational plan. Moreover, once the management program has been completed, it may not need complete redoing each year. However, a thorough analysis and review should be made annually to uncover any need for changes.

This focus on the management program should simplify the planning process. No matter what division of the planning process is decided on, however, enough time must be provided to deal with all phases of planning, including a necessarily somewhat complicated set of reviews and approvals. For a company operating on a calendar-year basis, a June-to-January planning cycle will be typical.

A written management program should be developed for each business and division, and for the company as a whole. The basic building block is the management program for each separate business, which should contain these sections or elements:

- Industry characteristics and outlook—with an assessment of the company's competitive position
- Corporate goals
- Major problems and opportunities
- Action programs for achieving goals, coping with problems, and exploiting opportunities
- Financial implications.

It should be kept in mind that the management program is not functionally organized—i.e., it is not concerned with marketing, engineering, and manufacturing individually. Typically, it will cover problems and opportunities that are far reaching enough to involve all functions. It is the operational plan that converts the broad over-all plans of the management program into specific plans and schedules for the individual functional departments—marketing, engineering, manufacturing, etc.

Thus the management program is cross-functional, while operating plans are usually functionally organized. It is in this phase of planning that alternatives are examined and decisions made on how resources are to be allocated to major programs, thus putting flesh on the bones of strategies and testing their feasibility.

Whereas the operating plan spells out the detailed steps for achieving the end result, the management program is typically summary in nature. For example, making a market survey of the 200 largest potential customers might be a major step in a program for increasing share-of-market. The management program would specify only the end result, the broad responsibility, and the final deadline; the operating plan would list all the principal steps needed to complete the survey and would fix responsibility and specify completion dates for each step.

Now—without going into the specific procedures that would be included in a planning guide—let's turn to the five sections or elements of a written management program and the types of information required in each.

Industry Outlook and Competitive Position

Industry characteristics and profit outlook, as well as the competitive position of each business, will have been analyzed in some detail during the preparation of strategic plans. In developing the management program, this prior analysis will be indispensable and should not be duplicated. However, the annual review and development of the management program require that line management (with assistance from the planning staff) again think deeply, creatively, and systematically about each business and the industry in which it operates.

Therefore, at least once a year there should be a careful analysis of any significant changes in the key factors for success in the industry—for example, new technological processes—and a review of trends that will enable top management to judge the long-term attractiveness of the industry. Such an analysis may show the need for further analysis or point up new ways of looking at the industry and the company's competitive position in it. It is all part of a continuous probing for a deeper understanding of the forces at work in the industry and their significance to the company.

To support these reviews, accurate trend data should be

accumulated to supplement and bring up to date the basic information gathered during the strategic planning phase. Where hard figures are not available, the best possible estimates should be made. Here are some examples of trend data that will typically need to be updated:

■ Growth (or decline) in industry volume—by products and market segments

■ Expansions and mergers of competitors

■ Industry capacity relative to demand

■ Industry cost and price trends

■ Industry return on investment

It is, of course, important to determine whether the industry is growing and at what rate, since that will largely determine the profit outlook for the business, division, and company.

Next, the competitive position of the business (or company) should be analyzed. This section of the management program should describe and document any significant trends in the domestic and worldwide competitive situation that could affect the outlook for the business and/or its profitability. Included should be significant factors such as these:

■ Trends in the business's share-of-market, broken down as much as possible by major product groups and market segments

■ Product-line and customer service strengths and weaknesses vis-à-vis competition, including specific advantages and disadvantages that might affect distributor actions or user buying decisions

■ Pricing strengths and weaknesses

In connection with user strategy, a competitive product-line/market evaluation should be made. Significant changes in customer positions that might affect the company's com-

petitive position in product performance, service, brand position, and price should be identified. Weaknesses in the product
line, as well as special advantages, should be pinpointed.

Finally, this section of the plan should be rounded out by
a written explanation summarizing the significant facts about
each business and pointing up significant trends in (1) market
makeup, size, and growth; (2) competitive volume, capacity,
and economic and cost position of the business in each major
market; and (3) the long-term profit outlook. This summary
should call attention to any special competitive advantages so
that these may be exploited, and to any special competitive
weaknesses, so these may be countered. Rather than merely
reciting the facts, it should highlight the changes that are
taking place, and their *significance*.

Goals

From the analysis of industry outlook and competitive position of the company, division, or business, quantitative goals
can be established as guides or targets for management and
operational planning.

Du Pont is notable for its pioneering in establishing a
high rate of return on investment as a primary goal for its
operating divisions, or industrial departments, as they are
called. This goal is a real challenge in divisional planning, because division managements know they will be judged by the
return shown by the operational plan and by the results recorded against the plan. The power of this approach was shown
by an incident a few years ago. On almost the same date that
another company announced its plan to build a new rayon
plant, Du Pont announced the liquidation of one of its rayon
plants, which had consistently fallen below its rate-of-return
goal.

However, other goals besides return on investment should probably be established. These include share-of-market, dollar sales volume, amount of capital employed, rate of growth in profits, growth in market value of common stock—even common stock price/earnings ratio. Whatever goals are used should be demanding but attainable. For, as Frederick R. Kappel, chairman of AT & T, has said, "A symptom of declining vitality is the failure to define new goals that are both meaningful and challenging." [2]

To make full use of the great integrating and optimizing values that flow from the profit-and-loss system (and thus avoid piecemeal management), some form of profit goal should be among those used for planning purposes. The value of a profit goal can be seen in one leading company that I have had opportunity to observe over many years. For nearly a decade one chief executive set increased sales volume as the goal for divisions, with secondary emphasis on profit. His target was to make the company a billion-dollar business before he retired— and he did it. His successor set a 10 percent annual increase in net profit per share as his goal. That goal was attained for 10 years, too.

Although the earlier volume goal had produced a significantly lower rate of return on investment, it was not for that reason wrong. Volume was extremely important in the economics of the business, especially at that period in the corporation's history. But the shift to a profit-growth goal did produce substantial changes in the way the business was operated: The divisions mounted specific programs to increase their share-of-market, cut manufacturing costs, reduce sales and advertising expense, and overhaul physical distribution. Some product lines were dropped and a few businesses liquidated. Profit growth accelerated, but growth in sales volume did slow down for a few years while the strategy conversion took place.

Valuable as profit goals (i.e., financial goals) may be, operating goals should not be neglected. For example, most successful managements keep a sharp eye on share-of-market and will not accept short-term profit at the expense of a declining share-of-market as satisfactory performance. Usually, it is wise to set multiple goals.

The choice of goals will, of course, depend on the particular situation. For example, the top management of a company with limited capital and/or management manpower should set goals that will require lower-level management to make sound choices in the use of scarce resources.

Which combination of goals will do most to ensure corporate success, and how goals shall be used, are decisions calling for top management's best skill and judgment in using its management system. These critical choices depend on the industry and its economics, the company's competitive position, the company's strategic plans, and many other factors. Although it is unwise to generalize about these choices, I can offer these guidelines distilled from the goal-setting experience of leading companies:

■ *Uses of goals.* The principal use of goals is to guide management programming and operational planning for the various businesses and divisions. The goals set by top management must be met before the plans will be acceptable. These goals are tied to strategy and help to achieve over-all company objectives. Goals will usually remain basically the same from year to year, but may be modified in order to carry out a particular strategy. Thus, a profit-rate goal may be lowered for a few years in order to achieve a significant increase in share-of-market.

Most divisional chief executives *want* corporate management to set goals. Over the years, division heads of major corporations have frequently made this type of complaint to me: "If top management would only tell us what they want us to do, then we could do it. As it is, we develop plans and they reject them as unsatisfactory. We'd save a lot of time, headaches, and frustration if we only had some guidelines from upstairs as to what *is* satisfactory. I just don't think top management is doing its job."

■ *Evaluation for goal-setting.* The choice of goals should not be made without a careful analysis of industry outlook, industry and company profit economics, company competitive position, and the possible effects of proposed goals on planning and other decision making in executing strategy. Goals are powerful motivators, and they should be established only after top management has carefully evaluated precisely what it wants accomplished.

■ *Number of goals.* A single goal—e.g., rate of return on investment—has the advantage of establishing a clear focus for planning. But it may also result in *short-term* planning, especially if management compensation and advancement are strongly influenced by short-term results. Operational goals used to supplement financial goals might include growth in sales volume and/or share-of-market, new account expansion, addition of critical manpower skills, improved manpower productivity, lowered costs, and the like.

Such goals should compel management to look behind financial indicators in order to ensure that any deterioration in the basic competitive position and operating performance of a company, division, or business will be recognized. For example, the profit-minded top management of a consumer packaged-goods company I know uses a profit goal combined with two other goals that oblige the divisions to watch what top management calls the "franchise health" of each major product group.

At the same time, too many goals can be confusing, and their guiding effect is largely dissipated. In a typical situation, perhaps two or three long-term goals might be established, with one or two shorter term goals designed to support a special strategy or meet particular conditions.

■ *Realism of goals.* Goals should balance realism with toughness. They should stretch executives but still be attainable. Unless they are demanding, they will fail to disturb the status quo. This is one of the reasons why it is so important that they should be based on a thorough factual analysis of industry and company economics and profit trends, competitive conditions, and the ways in which strategic plans can best be implemented.

These guidelines will help any management in setting goals. But there are, of course, no guidelines that can substitute for strategic thinking, skill, and judgment on management's part in using this powerful motivator and decision-making guide.

Major Problems and Opportunities

Every business always has major problems and major opportunities arising from external forces at work and from conditions within the company. And its success is always heavily influenced by how rapidly and effectively these are identified and acted on.

Under this approach to planning, the written management program should identify and specify ways of dealing with the most important of these problems and opportunities. In most cases, these will be generally known to executives at all levels; and probably they are dealing with them informally all the time. The reason for setting them down in the management program is to make sure that they are integrated in the planning and that action steps are developed to deal with them systematically rather than wait for a crisis.

It is not enough just to list and describe the major problems and opportunities. Each of them should also be quantified so that management can evaluate their relative importance and the amount of attention and resources that should be devoted to each. For example, a problem might be stated in such terms as these:

> The Martinsburg plant has excess capacity equivalent to $3,000,000 of sales (or a 20 percent increase). Achieving full utilization will also require an increase in plant personnel and other costs (exclusive of materials) of $750,000.

(*Not*, "The Martinsburg plant has excess capacity.")

A management program for one division stated its major problems like this:

1. Need to increase volume by about 30 percent in order to utilize capacity

2. Need to reduce production cost by 15 percent to be competitive in major markets and to lower the break-even point to 50 percent of capacity

3. Need to improve delivery performance and shorten delivery lead times by at least 20 percent in order to be fully competitive in the commercial vehicle market

4. Need to reduce total capital invested in the division by $1,500,000 in order to achieve the return-on-investment goal.

Requiring that major problems and opportunities be identified and quantified as specifically as this provides, in effect, another type of goal. Thus, in a divisionalized company, this approach to planning requires division management to bring to the attention of top management, with suggested action steps, all matters of major concern and all opportunities for major advances. Programs can then be developed to cope with the problems and to capitalize on the opportunities in the shortest feasible time. In this way, communications between corporate and division management can be concrete, meaningful, and constructive. This is one more way to take the "blue sky" out of planning.

Top management can assure an orderly approach to the identification and analysis of problems and opportunities by requiring that each type of strategy—user (product/market) strategy, profit strategy, and manpower strategy—be examined separately, as discussed in Chapter 3. Then the two or three most critical problems and opportunities in each area can be examined, and those most critical to total strategy chosen for management programming.

A few more illustrations may help to bring out the value of this simple problem/opportunity feature of the management program.

■ The management of a rapidly growing business knew it needed more working capital. Having decided not to borrow or sell additional stock, it mounted an intensive program for improved cash management. As a result, inventories, bank balances, and cash float were reduced sufficiently to free up several million dollars.

■ Some years ago a sharp drop (from 5 or 6 percent to 2 or 3 percent) in the annual growth rate of the petroleum business changed the economics of the industry. Low-cost refining and marketing became much more critical to success. One large company identified this change ahead of its competitors, analyzed its impact on profit strategy, and established a company-wide cost-reduction program that enabled it to continue its growth in earnings per share with little interruption. Meanwhile, its competitors suffered several years of declining profits.

■ The management of a new type of service business determined that it could preempt a commanding competitive position by being the first company to establish a worldwide network of administrative offices. To seize this opportunity, it set a goal each year for a specific number of new offices, accepting lower annual profits during the building period. Once the network was completed, profits shot up sharply and its dominant position was assured for some time.

Action Programs

The next section of the management program calls for broad but specific written programs (or sets of plans) for achieving the goals, coping with the problems, and exploiting the opportunities that have been identified for action. These individual programs also assign responsibilities and specify completion dates.

These broad but specific action plans are a vital feature of the management program. They are what distinguishes a management program from a mere forecast. Their nature and purpose are to make things happen. And this—as distinguished from *letting* things happen and then trying to cope with the consequences—is the crux of managing.

Indeed, the basic responsibility for managing the enterprise is focused in this feature of the management program. For the individual programs define, in accordance with the system, what is to be done, who is to do it, and what broad timetable is to be followed. (Near-term work schedules, as mentioned earlier, belong in the annual operating plan.)

Each problem or opportunity may require several separate programs. For example, a 10 percent reduction in manufacturing costs—needed to permit competitive pricing—might call for three separate programs: (1) improvements in material yield, (2) increased indirect labor productivity, and (3) reduction in final costs. Each of these programs would be quantified, broad responsibilities assigned, and the time of completion determined. Then each program would be further detailed and scheduled in the operating plan.

In developing programs, the analysis should be sufficiently penetrating to meet specific requirements. The opportunity should be quantified—e.g., in terms of target savings against which progress can be measured. And the steps needed to achieve these results should be explicitly spelled out.

Whenever possible, alternative action programs should be offered to provide management with a choice as to how a goal is to be reached, a problem solved, or an opportunity seized. The pros and cons of each alternative should be clear enough to enable top management to evaluate the program or set of programs presented for review.

The value of this kind of specific planning is easy to appreciate. Yet not many companies have done it successfully. Some have been frightened off by the detail; others have gotten bogged down in it. Of course, the key is to strike the right balance between too much and too little detail. Too much can cause the whole effort to fall of its own weight; too little provides no useful guide for action and no basis for evaluating the adequacy of the plan or for measuring results against it.

In striking this balance, only enough information should be provided to answer the five questions that any management must ask when it reviews an individual action program:

■ Why and how will each program help us to deal with the problem or opportunity?

■ Among the alternatives offered, which is the best program to deal with the problems and opportunities?

- How significant a contribution will each program make, e.g., what will its profit impact be?
- What *major* steps must be taken by what key executives to carry out each action program?
- How soon will each action program be completed?

If the executives and supervisors who must cooperate in carrying out a program are all in the same organizational unit, then less detail will be required. And top management needs only enough detail to be sure that implementation of the total management program has been thought through and will be effective. No great amount of detail is required to put a program in shape for use as a basis of measurement, unless the quantified targets and time specifics (the real heart of a program) are considered "detail."

Of course, operating personnel are responsible for the final details required to carry out each step; and that level of detail is not part of the management program nor even of the operating plan. In fact, most of the final detailing of action is never written out at all.

Only through experience in each division or company can the correct balance of detail in the management plan be worked out. The necessity for learning by experience how to develop and simplify the planning procedure is one reason why it takes so long to establish an effective planning program. However, as I have tried to show, the pay-off from planning makes the effort worthwhile. No frontier effort is ever easy.

Financial Implications

The final section of the management program summarizes the financial implications of the programs that make it up, and provides a measure of the extent to which they help achieve the goals that have been established. The information summarized in this section should answer questions such as these:

- Will the programs attain established goals? Are the goals adequate? Are the goals too demanding?

- Is there a significant profit improvement over past performance?

- What additional funds will be required?

The financial department—that is, the controller and treasurer—has an important role in planning, which includes:

- Providing information on the financial implications of the management program and the operational plan. This is information that others need in their planning.

- Preparing plans for generating the cash or credit necessary to finance management programs and operating plans.

- Preparing the plans for its own sections—e.g., accounting, credit, and tax.

- Assisting generally in all phases of planning.

The financial department provides four principal kinds of information for the final section of the management program.

Profit projections: These are statements projecting profit and loss two to six years ahead, based on projected or assumed sales volume. The reasons should be stated for any expected changes in profits or in return on investment, including the relative profit significance of the individual programs that make up the complete management program.

As noted earlier, these profit-and-loss projections should be prepared no further ahead than is realistically feasible and necessary for plans that must be carried forward. For example, a major program involving substantial capital expenditures may call for five-year projections of capital requirements; this can usually be done in a meaningful way.

Trend data: There should be tables showing historical and projected trends in key financial indicators, such as sales volume, orders on hand, cost of goods sold, operating profit, number of employees, and return on investment.

Capital needs: Known capital needs for the coming years should be broken down by type—e.g., funds for expansion, replacement, and cost reduction. And there should be a review of the results achieved on any major capital expenditures, by type, during the past two or three years.

Break-even data: It is useful to include a break-even chart showing the current impact of volume, price, and product mix on profits, since it will help everyone understand the profit economics of the business.

Thus this final section helps top management evaluate the action features of the over-all management program.

Challenging Programs and Plans

This approach to planning enables top management to get forward control of the division or company through its own participation in the early phases of the planning process, followed by top-management review and approval of each subsequent phase. Thus, top management is initially responsible for setting or approving objectives and goals and for approving strategy. In the final stages, it again steps in to review the management program and operating plans and budgets and determine whether they do carry out approved strategy and will achieve established goals.

This approach takes top management out of the relatively helpless position of considering only a single operating budget, which often lacks qualitative support. Of course, if top management does not like the projected results, it can always send the budget back to be "worked over." But in doing so, management puts itself in the posture of an antagonistic negotiator vis-à-vis those who are recommending the operating budget.

Better results will be obtained if, under the planning approach I have described, the management program is presented in several alternative forms—or at least with sufficient qualitative information so that top management is not faced with a forced choice. Each alternative should be costed out and its volume, profit, and manpower consequences expressed in quantified terms with qualitative support. Of course one of the alternatives should be recommended. Then, with intelligible choices before it, top management can really participate and gain effective forward control.

Moreover, top management and the recommending executives will be on the same side of the table. Instead of negotiating as antagonists, they will be deciding together, on a factual basis, what will be best for the business. After examining each alternative, top management can approve one, suggest a combination of two, or turn down all the proposals and ask that more planning be done.

This approach works best if it focuses on the management program. An approved management program provides an approved planning base (or groundwork) for preparing the annual operating plan, thus saving substantial time in reviews and revisions at the later and more detailed stage of planning.

This kind of planning and review not only produces the best results but also creates the best morale. Top management can participate effectively and decide factually. The recommending executives are put in a more dignified position; they are not trying to "sell" a budget or "get it by" top management. If their work has been thorough and factual and their planning assumptions sound, top-management approval does not put them out on a limb. Indeed, if there should be a change in the facts on which an approved program, plan, or budget was based, they can, without fear, come back to top management with a new plan based on the new facts.

In this way, top management teams up with lower-level management to decide on the course of action that—in the light of the existing external and internal facts—can *influence the future* to the company's best advantage. Top management will not then be surprised by sudden new developments. Nor will it permit the business simply to drift with the forces at work in the environment.

Annual Operating Plan

Once the management program has been approved, the rest of the planning process (i.e., preparing the annual operating plan and capital budgets) is a good deal easier. In fact, the annual operating plan is simply a detailing and scheduling of that part of the management program which is to be carried out during the next operating year. Consequently, a well-prepared management program not only provides the groundwork for the annual operating plan but includes most of the other information as well.

Operating plans typically take one of two forms:

■ One form resembles the management program, except that it is more detailed. It includes a schedule or timetable of events, by department, covering each phase of the program. An operating plan of this type prepared by one company consists of a series of departmental schedules, each with columns headed "Description of Program," "Steps," "Responsibility and Timing," "Profit Impact," and "Progress."

Thus each department draws on the management program to decide how its activities are to be carried on during the year ahead. Since over-all strategy is unlikely to change frequently, not many departments will make major changes in direction in a single year. But the goals that have been set should require each department to develop plans that will improve its performance in some specified manner. In one company, for example, every department head right down to the foreman is required to have specific annual plans for improving performance *and* reducing cost.

When an operating plan of this type has been developed, the individual plans are then converted into the annual operating budget and any capital budgets. Finally, the operating plan and the resulting budgets are presented to top management for review and approval.

■ The second type of operating plan also includes the actions necessary to implement the management program, but takes a different form. Instead of a program orientation alone, it consists of a pyramid of departmental, divisional, and company plans, as well as business and/or product-line plans—all supported in detail with schedules and quantitative data. These individual plans, and their supporting detail, are then reflected in the annual operating budget and capital budgets for the division or company as a whole; and these are presented to top management for review and approval.

The figures for sales volume and profit used in *any* type of annual operating plan are, of course, goals and not forecasts. The executives who recommend them thereby commit themselves to achieve these results, and their plans are designed accordingly. Thus the company refuses to be a victim of its environment. By committing itself to achieve specified goals, it takes command of the future instead of merely predicting it.

The annual operating plan, at the action end of the planning spectrum, should be understandable, specific, and attainable—but also demanding. And, prepared in the way I have described, every action it calls for will be geared to the user, profit, and manpower strategies on which the management program is based.

Thus the operating plan wraps up the whole system of management for the year ahead and provides specific guidelines for departmental and sectional action. In doing so it integrates and energizes the whole system. At the same time, the management system itself—through its philosophy, policies, standards, and organizational assignments of responsibility and authority— guides the responsible managers in carrying out the annual plan. All these components interact to produce the multiplier effect of the system approach to managing an enterprise.

Planning Staff

The role of the corporate (or divisional) planning director has already been discussed, but a few further comments about him and his small staff may be in order here.

I believe that the title of the staff director should include the word "corporate" or "divisional," as the case may be. This will help convey the fact that this staff is concerned with *overall* company or division planning. The point is important, because *every* executive must plan. The corporate planning director cannot do it for him, and should not try.

The planning staff helps the line managers with all phases of planning: strategic, management, and operational. It gathers and analyzes facts and puts tentative programs and plans in shape for consideration by line managers. The staff keeps up to date on industry trends and competitive conditions, which are essential background for both strategic and management planning. It gathers and analyzes information from outside the business, as well as from marketing, financial, and other executives within the company.

But the planning staff should not do the planning work of line managers. It should work *with* the line, not *for* the line. Such a relationship enables the staff not only to make planning suggestions to the line but to challenge line executives' assumptions and conclusions in the planning decisions that *they* must make.

Control

Planning and control go together like love and marriage. In fact, some students of management argue that it is impossible to separate them. I believe the separation is not only possible but desirable.

Nature of control: Some years ago an officer of Marks & Spencer, Britain's largest chain of clothing and food stores, took me through an exhibit they maintained in their London headquarters. It was a "before-and-after" exhibit to show how they had overhauled their control system.

The "before" part of the exhibit showed hundreds of complex forms designed to gather enormous quantities of data and other information in minute detail. The forms were assembled and labeled in such a way that even quick inspection showed how ineffectual, costly, and even silly the whole system had been. The "after" part of the exhibit showed a vastly reduced number of forms. Each form in the complete new set was simple, providing only obviously necessary and usable information.

The exhibit was designed to make a strong impact, and it achieved its goal. There, laid out in one room, were the forms for "controlling" the buying and resale of thousands of items of merchandise through hundreds of stores; for building stores; for hiring, evaluating, advancing, and paying thousands of men and women from the chief executive to sales clerks; and for carrying on all the other activities of a vast and intricate business.

All those forms did—all they could do—was to *present in-formation.* Of course, the purpose of the information was to stimulate and guide *management decision making and action.* For example, if the information showed excessive inventories, then buying would be slowed down, a sale would be held, or plans would otherwise be changed. If it indicated violations of policy, some corrective or disciplinary action would be taken.

In this sense the control component is strictly an information component. True, the information it provides is designed to induce action. But the action does not follow automatically from the information. If it did, there would be no need for capable managers. The information simply influences managerial will, judgment, and initiative—and the managers take whatever action they deem appropriate in the circumstances. In a sense, that is what management is all about. That is why I consider inducing action a separate component and reserve it for Chapter 8 (the next and final chapter).

Actually, the term "control" itself is somewhat misleading, since control involves changing people's behavior by motivating them in some way. Therefore, I think it may be more helpful to give up the concept of "control" as a component in favor of two separate components: *management information* and *activating people.* (In any case, the classic notion of control is wholly contrary to the concept of *self*-control for which I argue in Chapter 8.)

Once we focus on the concept of *management information,* we can approach the task simply and directly. What management needs to activate and reactivate people is (1) information on which to base planning, (2) measures of performance of the people involved, and (3) feedback on what is actually happening. This planning information/performance measurement/information feedback cycle is an *information* cycle. It provides the basis for action—not the action itself.

Is "controller" the right title? I find the management information notion so valuable in making the will to manage effective that I'm even inclined to question the advisability of the title "controller" that is now so common in U.S. companies. The controller *function,* of course, is a highly useful one that has made a great contribution to management effectiveness. Indeed, as mentioned earlier, the treasurer and controller (i.e., the finance department) have a unique and important role in the whole planning process. They have an equally important role in making other parts of the system effective. But the connotation of the *title* "controller" is, to my mind, unfortunate.

For the controller *should not control.* Of course he has functional authority to see that accounting and other procedures are followed. But beyond that, his role is to supply management information, analyze that information, and advise the line on what action is indicated. That is not controlling. Controlling, in the sense defined earlier, is the job of the line executives, who do it by activating people in some way.

When a controller over-reaches the information function and actually exercises control—as some do—it is neither good for the company nor good for the controller himself in his relations with the line. Perhaps his title subtly encourages the controller to over-reach his authority. That may be the reason why a few companies (General Motors among them) still use the former title "comptroller."

At any rate, I believe that "Director of Management Information and Analysis," or simply "Director of Management Information," would be a more accurate title for the controller. It would remind the man who holds the job (and everyone else) just what his role is and how he should approach his job. Hence it might encourage many controllers to increase their contributions and therefore their value to the company.

Approach to supplying management information: The task of the Director of Management Information, then, is to supply information that will enable managers and supervisors to manage the company in accordance with the management system. Specifically, information will be needed for:

1. Establishing objectives, developing strategy, and setting goals

2. Formulating policies

3. Developing management plans, operating plans, operating budgets, and capital budgets

4. Making specific decisions

5. Evaluating the need for changing any of the foregoing or for activating people to change their performance, based on new facts, new judgments, performance measures, and information feedback.

Managers need information on *actual* performance so they can compare it with *planned* performance—and so they can assess the adequacy of performance and the appropriateness of the original objectives, strategy, goals, policies, plans, and budgets. Thus feedback and performance measurement are needed to inform managers whether any inadequate performance is due to the plan or to the man.

When conceived in this fashion, the management information component takes on new simplicity. In applying this approach to control, however, a number of points should be kept in mind.

First, since management information is collected only to serve as a guide to decision making and action, it is wasteful and frustrating to prepare more information than can or will be used. Most managements would find the preparation of a forms exhibit like Marks & Spencer's a sobering experience. In thousands of companies, millions of pounds of unread paper are being prepared and stored in expensive space to frustrate hundreds of thousands of managers and supervisors who wish they had time to read it but know subconsciously it would be futile to do so.

The computer offers the promise of saving managers from inundation in this sea of paper. The procedure analysis that must precede computer programming usually results in worthwhile simplification by itself. On the other hand, the computer's enormous capacity to spew out data makes it easy to demand "more"—a temptation that must be resisted.

Second, since the purpose of management information is to help managers make decisions and activate people, it should be presented in terms of units of responsibility. This well-established principle is too frequently overlooked or ignored. The computer can help make it effective in many businesses.

Third, management information can be reduced in quantity and increased in quality if it is supplied to each manager and supervisor in terms of the key factors determining the successful performance of his particular job. The sales manager of a very large and complex region of a major company found that eight key figures from a computer, replacing more than 170 forms, gave him all the information he needed. Management information should be shaped to the needs of the individual user—i.e., the kinds of decisions and actions he can actually take. These should determine the content and terminology of the report, its time-frame (the period covered), its frequency, currency, and form (narrative, numerical, or graphic).

Information for measuring performance against plan can be further simplified if data not relevant to the key factors are eliminated. Key factors should be identified during the planning process, particularly in the course of preparing the management program. Then they should be highlighted in the operating plan, becoming the basic measures of performance.

Fourth, the management information system should, of course, incorporate the principle of reporting by exception. Thus, favorable as well as unfavorable deviations from the operating plan and budget should be brought to the attention of the responsible executives. Again, the computer will help make this principle a reality.

Fifth, for the purpose of making decisions and taking action, financial information, while essential, is often less useful and timely than operating information. Financial information usually cannot be provided so quickly. Often, too, it does not come in a form on which to base decisions and action. Here again the computer can help.

Sixth, basically the computer system should be oriented to providing operating as well as financial information. Some chief executives have taken computer system design and even computer operation away from treasurers and controllers because these financially oriented executives have not been sufficiently responsive to the operating information needs of line managers and supervisors. The computer is such an enormously valuable management information tool that no company can afford to use it solely as a bookkeeping machine.

Organization practice in fixing responsibility and authority for computer management is still in a state of ferment. The best way to organize this activity varies, of course, with company circumstances. But it is important to recognize that in every case four kinds of responsibility are involved: (1) deciding what information is to be supplied by the computer, (2) designing the computer system to provide it, (3) programming the computer, and (4) operating the computer.

The first two responsibilities are the most critical. They should be assigned with care, because both tasks must be approached with the determination that the computer shall provide useful, timely, and understandable information for decision making and action at all levels of management.

A simple and basic approach to making business plans and supplying information for management decision and action holds great promise for even the best-managed companies. The revolution in planning and management information is still in its early stages. But it is already becoming trite to observe that the computer is turning that revolution into an explosion.

Planning and management information in the simple but fundamental form discussed here should be integral parts of every successful management system. In that way they can energize and integrate the whole system and provide the multiplier effect of interactions among the various system components.

However, every system of management must meet the ultimate test of how effectively it causes people to decide and act. This final test of an effective management system is discussed in the next and last chapter.

8

Activating People: The "Let's Go" Component of the System

A few years ago a society I belong to helped defray the travel expenses of a group of Swiss educators who were touring the United States to study our educational system. When they got back home, one of them—a school principal—wrote us a long letter of thanks. In it he said:

> The love of you Americans for industrial organization is not love of wealth but the pleasure of achievement. You take delight in producing bigger and better things, in inventing more ingenious contrivances, in discovering ways of harnessing nature. No wonder there is such a close association between industry and culture in your country!

Even discounting the natural tendency of a grateful guest to say nice things, I believe that Swiss principal has captured something important in the spirit of America. Most Americans do inherently want to work—and work productively. Many work for the "pleasure of achievement," as the principal put it. But many more must be motivated in other ways. And even those who want to work must be purposefully activated.

Activating as a System Component

To be effective, the will to manage must ultimately be reflected in the purposeful and productive actions of people.

Therefore, an effective system for managing a company must activate the people in it to perform the work required in a purposeful and productive manner.

The word "activate" may seem pretty stuffy. All it means is "to make active"—in other words, to get people going. There are many ways to get people going: order them, impose penalties on them, advise them, encourage them, frighten them, drive them, lead them, inspire them, grant them rewards, motivate them in other ways, and—best of all—let them govern themselves, i.e., use self-direction and self-control. In making his will to manage effective, every manager must—in some situation—use all these ways in varying combinations or packages, and no word but "activate" seems to cover them all.

I believe that the activating package will be most effective when it is part of the management system. In fact, the interdependencies and interrelationships of the various means for activating people underscore the value of the systems approach to managing. When individual activating methods are integral parts of a total system, they support one another and draw strength from other system components. In short, the total interaction makes the activating task easier and more effective.

I have already discussed the *managing processes* that stimulate a man to perform productively: letting him feel the full weight of responsibility through real delegation of authority, letting him know where he stands and how he is doing, levelling with him about how he can improve his performance, offering advancement opportunities, and compensating him properly. There are eight principal *means* of activating a person to work productively as part of the system of management:

1. Orders
2. Penalties
3. Advice

4. Constructive job attitudes
5. Rewards
6. Personal commitment
7. Self-government
8. Leadership.

Note that the first seven of these form a spectrum, ranging from strong discipline at one end to self-government at the other. The eighth, leadership, complements them all. It minimizes the need for orders and penalties, creates constructive job attitudes, uses rewards, develops personal commitments to the purposes and philosophy of the company, and stimulates self-government.

Because I believe that maximum self-government activates people to turn out the most work, that is discussed first. Then I consider each of the other ways to "get people going." Finally, I take up the ways in which an executive can use each of these activating means as part of the management system to bring about purposeful and productive action.

Self-government

Doctors, ministers, teachers, artists, authors, and other *individual* professional men are necessarily self-governing, and they succeed or fail accordingly. Most of the outstanding ones work with great dedication and productivity: a Leonardo da Vinci, a Hemingway, or a Thomas Edison. Similarly, the individual business proprietor must govern himself. Ordinarily, the more effectively he puts out the greater his success is likely to be. The challenge in managing groups is to find ways to develop the same kind of productive effectiveness by creating, for each key man in the organization, a situation approximating that of the responsible individual proprietor.

In the best law firms, that situation is substantially achieved and self-government is virtually a reality. The young lawyers recruited by leading firms are carefully selected men of high caliber. They come educated in the law; self-disciplined to advise clients on the law as laid down by statute, regulation, and the courts; dedicated to the law; and motivated to succeed professionally by serving clients well. On joining such a firm the young lawyer quickly learns that the philosophy of his firm requires him to observe high ethical and professional standards and to dedicate himself to his clients' interests.

Thus, leading law firms have a sort of automatic, built-in system of management, though they do not call it that. Several components of the system are developed by the man's law school training and brought into the firm when he joins. Much of the balance of the system is inherent in the firm's philosophy. Self-government follows naturally as each lawyer attracts clients or receives assignments. Senior supervising lawyers offer advice, criticism, and occasionally praise. Always there is the challenge of the work and the satisfaction of knowing that the client has been served well—especially when the client himself says so.

Always operating as positive incentives are group approval and the year-end bonus, large or small. More specific negative incentives are the potential disapproval of seniors and the ever-present though unmentioned up-or-out policy requiring separation of the man who has not been advanced to partnership within a generally understood period or set of conditions.

But in the large law firm, orders are rarely given. No one drives the lawyer except himself; and, typically, the standards of performance he sets for himself are far higher than anyone would even consider imposing on him. Leadership involves no waving of arms or pounding of desks; it is exercised chiefly by example. The seniors are generally so respected outside and inside the firm that the young lawyers observe their methods closely and try to emulate them.

I don't mean that large law firms couldn't be better managed. But I have observed that professional men who work in groups to earn a profit—lawyers, accountants, and management consultants—work more productively than any businessmen except those who manage their own businesses, and some top management executives of the most successful American corporations. Certainly the professional man who is largely activated by self-direction and self-control works more productively than the typical business executive.

By productivity, I don't mean hard work in the sense of long hours. The typical American executive knows no office hours, and the fat briefcase merely transfers his work to his home. I mean "productive" in terms of accomplishment: purposeful, effective, and satisfying work in carrying out the strategy of the company and otherwise contributing to company success (as measured by volume and share-of -market, return on investment, and continuity of effective management).

As a close observer of professional firms and business concerns, I believe that any business can approach the productivity of the professional firm by developing and using its own tailor-made system of programmed management—a system that will enable it to activate its people more powerfully through greater use of self-government.

Of course, you'll think immediately that the small size of the professional firm makes self-government more feasible—and of course you'll be right. But I submit, nevertheless, that a well-developed system of management—consistently supported by good, not necessarily brilliant, leadership—can enable a business of any size to attain a considerable degree of self-direction and self-control. And the business that does employ self-government to activate its people will be substantially more effective than those which rely more heavily on the other means of activation. I can't prove this, but I believe it deeply.

Self-government, of course, is most important for executives and supervisors. The higher an executive's position, the more self-government he should be expected to exercise. But experience shows that in a soundly managed business, a well-selected and well-led group of stenographers will turn out better work, and more of it, if they are activated more by self-control than by strict discipline and detailed direction. Union regulations aside, the same applies to a group of manual workers in a plant.

Most people want or can be persuaded to work productively. Confidential discussions over the years have convinced me that most men, even on the lower executive levels, really like to work. Most would like to work more productively. Most executives and supervisors regard work as a source of satisfaction and they perform it eagerly.

Business executives, like professional men, will put out more if they are permitted self-direction and self-control in achieving objectives and goals to which they are committed. But they must believe that what the company is doing is worthwhile and that their own efforts are directly related to the accomplishments of the company. Many conversations with executives in a wide range of businesses have persuaded me that most men in responsible positions seldom fully utilize their potential—much to their frustration. They would like to exercise more responsibility and use more of their capacity for analytical and creative work if only management methods would *allow* them to—or, better yet, if only management methods, working climate, and executive actions would *encourage* them to do so. I believe that any business will enjoy greater success if its managing processes and managing actions are based on these principles.

The need for freedom of the individual in business is widely recognized. In an election speech in Britain during the 1964 campaign, Prime Minister Sir Alec Douglas-Home said:

Now that our national livelihood depends on holding our own in a scientific and mechanical age, the case for giving the individual full scope for his talent is overwhelming. The young generation will rise to opportunity, but we shall never get the best out of them through direction and orders.

Crawford Greenewalt, chairman of Du Pont, applied the need for freedom even more broadly when he spoke on the occasion of the 150th anniversary of J. P. Stevens & Company:

Give men the maximum of freedom, the maximum of incentive, and the achievements of the individual will be fused into the accomplishment of the institution.

I think there can be no question that the long-time success of the Stevens Company has been due to the precepts articulated in our national being, applied to the needs of an industrial organization: maximum freedom, maximum incentive, creating between them an environment in which each individual gives of his best.

But the top managers of a company must build a framework for action before they can get out of the way and let the people go to it. A system for managing provides that framework, and leadership can supply whatever additional activating may be needed. Thus, effective self-government *requires* precisely the elements that a system of management *provides:*

- Strategic plans, effectively articulated, that make clear to everyone the objectives of the business and the strategies for attaining them

- A philosophy of management to provide powerful, over-riding beliefs in "the way we do things around here"

- A plan of organization to define the activities to be performed and the authority needed to get those things done

- Policies, standards, and procedures to provide guidelines for action in carrying out strategy

■ Operating plans and management control processes to provide information for decision making and for guiding action into the most productive and profitable channels

■ Activation to whatever degree is necessary to make people most purposefully productive.

Such a framework, neither too detailed nor too restrictive, provides guidance, not direction. The range for individual decision and action is broad, and self-direction and self-control can still thrive. A minimum of advice and penalties will be needed. Motivation will be largely centered in the challenge and satisfaction of a job well done. And leadership will be needed chiefly for articulating the objectives and goals, setting an example, and maintaining a stimulating work climate.

Granted, full self-government in business is an ideal only. In practice, it can be attained only to a degree in some companies and in parts of many companies. But I do believe that considerable self-government is entirely practical in *every* company. And a substantial degree of self-government is so profitable a target that it is well worth shooting for.

Compared with European businesses, most American companies already have a large element of self-government. Perhaps this is because, as Mr. Greenewalt indicated, our business methods incorporate in some measure the spirit of the American Revolution as reflected in the Declaration of Independence and the Constitution. You will recall also the specific reference to a "democratic system" in the Jersey Standard statement of management principles I quoted earlier.

In any event, European business practice typically calls for stricter control and more detailed instructions from the top. As European companies expand in size and complexity under the influence of the Common Market, competition will doubtless force the larger enterprises to develop management methods that will permit and encourage a much greater degree of self-government. Detailed direction from the top can never produce such effective and profitable results for large-scale enterprises as can management methods that encourage self-direction and self-control.

In and out of business, people instinctively like freedom. Given freedom within a framework for guiding their actions, accompanied by good leadership, most people will accept responsibility and exercise initiative and imagination. They will set high standards for themselves, and they will work harder, longer, and more productively to meet those standards.

Progressive U.K. and European companies are already vitally interested in adopting American management methods. An essential part of that adaptation will inevitably be more individual self-government through adoption of American business practices such as divisionalization, greater delegation, and less rigid control.

Perhaps the most striking evidence of the usefulness of self-government is the spread of "consultative" or "participative" management in American business. More and more, people are asked by their superiors to take a hand in shaping the policies, plans, and programs that will govern their later actions. Not only does this improve the quality of the policies, plans, and programs, but it motivates people to carry them out more effectively and more willingly, thus making self-government more feasible. So I'm urging every company to shoot for the star of individual self-government. Even if the effort falls short (as it will), the company will still be more successful and more profitable.

Consider another example. After the unexpected death of the dominant chief executive, a relatively young vice president was advanced to the presidency of his company, a leader in a highly competitive industry. During the next two years, the level of general business remained stable and the company made no major changes in product line, prices, plants, marketing policies, or executive personnel. Yet the company's competitive position was strengthened; its volume and share-of-market increased; and its earnings per share *doubled*.

When I asked how it all happened, the new chief executive said, "I just gave people their heads." Actually that was just what had happened. He had *ordered* them less than his predecessor, and *controlled* them less. People at all levels were freer to do what they had wanted to do all along. The same people simply worked more effectively—and with more zest—in carrying out substantially the same operating program with precisely the same plan of organization. A board of directors that was thinking of selling the business found instead that the company had the management resources to successfully acquire others.

G. K. Chesterton said, "The Christian ideal has not been tried and found wanting. It has been found difficult, and left untried." The same is true of self-government in business. For the most part, it too has been left untried. But when it *has* been tried, it has not been found wanting.

Since no ideal is fully attainable, every manager will have to make some use of the other principal ways of activating people to work productively in a system-managed company. So let's look at each of these in turn.

Orders

Response to an order—i.e., action taken by one person in response to the command of another in higher authority—is at the opposite end of the activation spectrum from self-government. Not often in business do we hear the military phrase, "That is an order." Executives are more likely to couch their commands as requests or suggestions, which are understood as orders and acted on accordingly.

Because they lack a system of management that makes orders less necessary, most companies today are closer to the imposed discipline end of the activation spectrum than to the self-government end. You may recall my case example of the chief executive who was so dominant and imposed such strong discipline that people in the business tried to guess his wishes and obey them. I know from talking with people at all levels in that company that they would have been much more productive if they had been freer to think and act on their own. They would have exercised more initiative and imagination, set higher performance standards for themselves, and just plain worked harder if they had not been perpetually waiting for orders.

Here are some further illustrations of disciplinary restrictions on the profitable activation of people:

■ One highly disciplined business is having difficulty recruiting men from graduate business schools. One or two from each school join and then leave in a few years. After that, others can't be recruited for two or three years. The reason is that campus feedback gives the company poor marks as a place to work: "Don't go there unless you just want to take orders."

■ In another highly disciplined business, even high-level executives don't dare to disagree with top management; instead, they carry out programs in which they don't believe. As one vice president put it to me, "I'm not going to stick my neck out." Thus, top management denies itself the benefit of additional facts and the critical judgments of highly qualified men. At the same time, it incurs the inevitable penalties of higher cost and lower effectiveness in the execution of programs about which there is skepticism.

■ Before a change in the chief executive of a large, highly disciplined variety chain, store managers throughout the country carried merchandise that they knew would sell poorly and followed practices that they knew were not suited to their particular stores. Their reasoning: "I don't want to get clobbered. Let them find out for themselves that the stuff won't sell."

■ Executives in a large metal-working business are currently waiting for an order-giving chief executive to retire so their freedom will be restored. If he were not nearing retirement age, many able executives would follow the one who left recently saying, "I can't take it for even a few years more."

Executives in a highly disciplined business are like the troops in Tennyson's "Charge of the Light Brigade": "Theirs not to reason why, theirs but to do and die." When that is the attitude of any executive or supervisor, profits are bound to suffer. Facts will be suppressed or not brought to the higher-level decision maker. Initiative will be dulled. Top management will be denied the benefits of the imagination and creativity of people close to the scene of action. People will work only to imposed standards, doing only what they have to. Feedback from down the line to correct errors in policies, procedures, and programs will be scanty and slow in coming. The enthusiasm and spirit that increase effectiveness and cut costs will be missing. The zest for work that stimulates high-caliber men to put out will be lacking.

To be sure, in every situation short of the ideal, orders will from time to time be necessary. However, the temptation to rely too heavily on orders is always strong, because the command is an easy managing tool for anyone in authority to use: just *tell* the person. Study and observation convince me, however, that orders should be used so sparingly and so deftly—at least in business— that they can be questioned by the person commanded whenever he has a factual or even an intuitive objection. Certainly, orders should not be so compelling, arbitrary, or forceful that they dull the enthusiasm of those commanded or restrict the feedback from below. With programmed management, good leaders will need to make only limited use of orders.

Penalties

No system of management can operate effectively without penalties imposed or threatened. Even with a high degree of self-government, there is always some threat of penalty in the background, if only the threat that self-government will be taken away if it proves ineffective.

In a system-managed business, however, penalties are less necessary and the system gives leverage to those that must be imposed. Even potential group disapproval becomes a powerful motivating force.

Other than that, the chief penalties best suited to a system-managed business are—in order of increasing severity—reprimand, reduction or elimination of supplemental compensation, delay in advancement, and dismissal for continued poor performance. Some companies use the threat of early retirement at a reduced pension as a means for maintaining the level of performance of older executives.

Because of human frailty, even the extreme penalty of dismissal must be available to management. Dismissal of poor performers early in their careers will put iron into the system without being unfair to the man. I have seen many poor performers kept on in important positions. Such cases are tragic for the man as well as for the company, because he might have done well somewhere else if he had been dismissed while he could still get another executive job.

Imposed with fairness and consideration, executive penalties constitute an important activating means in any company. A good leader will impose them sparingly, but without hesitation when they are required. A tough manpower policy elicits the loyalties of the capable people—and fairly administered in the right circumstances, it improves the morale of the people who count.

A system-managed business has less need for penalties, because the interaction of system guidelines and components requires less personal activation by executives and supervisors. But the velvet glove of self-direction and self-control must always be ready, when necessary, to grasp and use the little stick of minor penalties, and ultimately the big stick of replacement.

When he was vice president of GM and general manager of the Chevrolet Division, Semon E. Knudsen made a speech to a group of students at the Graduate School of Business Administration at Michigan University. In it he said:

> In business, threat and incentive work hand in hand to keep a man up to his best performance.
>
> The threat is veiled in opportunity. Let a man do his job his own way as long as he is successful; if he fails, be tough-minded enough to replace him.[1]

Advice

Advice or suggestions are, of course, used extensively to activate people. Under a sound system for managing, a suggestion will not be received as an order. Advice is always more palatable than an order, simply because the recipient feels free to accept or reject the suggestion. And because it is closer to the self-government end of the activating spectrum than an order, advising is a more profitable way to activate.

The programmed management system permits advice to be used in at least three organizational relationships:

1. Every superior advises his subordinates. That is, he makes

suggestions (including coaching suggestions) that are so clearly short of orders that they are understood as advice. This is the most important and most common advisory relationship in business.

2. Functional executives make suggestions that are not intended to carry functional authority.

3. Staff executives and staff workers do nothing but develop and offer advice except as they may occasionally exercise authority specifically delegated by a line superior.

For advice to flourish in a company and become valuable through action, a spirit of open-mindedness is essential. Fortunately, this spirit is encouraged by a company philosophy that establishes the fact-founded approach to decision making and creates a climate of objectivity.

A skillful advisor is perceptive about the situation and sensitive to the attitudes of the person he is advising. He senses not only the other man's normal viewpoints, prejudices, and ways of acting, but also the particular conditions affecting his personal situation at the time: his power strengths and weaknesses, his personal political position, and other factors affecting both his willingness and his ability to act on the advice. And the skillful advisor will make certain that what is *meant* as advice is so understood.

Advice is a useful activating tool. In a company that manages by system, it can be used freely to replace orders and to help improve self-directed performance.

Constructive Job Attitudes

Constructive job attitudes, which are essential to maximum productive individual performance, stem largely from the way the business is managed. Hence, the principal keys to these attitudes have already been discussed. But understanding the specific reasons why men like or dislike their jobs will help a manager to increase individual productivity.

Assuming fair compensation—constructive job attitudes result chiefly from three factors: (1) freedom of the individual to act on his own, (2) opportunity to advance on the basis of performance, and (3) sense of achievement.

Freedom to act independently: In discussing "executive attitudes" in his speech to the graduate business students at Michigan University, Semon Knudsen said:

> A business will progress in direct ratio to the intellectual freedom of action given to the executives in its organization.
>
> By no means do I suggest that individuality run rampant over organizational purpose.
>
> The structure may be constant—and must continue—but its function is made up of hundreds of separate jobs. It is the successful accomplishment of the separate task, rather than the techniques used to approach it, that should be the criterion. Responsibility, authority, and the right to individual method must go hand in hand. . . .
>
> The important thing to the organization is that each man be given the opportunity to exploit his talent to the fullest in the way best suited to his personality.

Here we see the influence of the management system in creating constructive job attitudes: Organization structure fixes responsibility, delegation of authority grants freedom, and these two managing processes combine to facilitate "individual method" in working toward "organizational purpose."

Mr. Knudsen's observation that the "right to individual method" is fundamental to constructive job attitudes is supported by a good many comments from the men who participated in my high-talent survey (described in Chapter 6). Here are some of the answers they gave to my question, "Why have you stayed with your present company?"

"An atmosphere that makes the qualified individual feel he is his own boss."

"Damn fine training. Yet excellent company attitude toward letting individual work his own way."

"Given responsibility—great variety in work—great freedom in scheduling and carrying out my work—chance to do some creative work."

"Men are given the authority as well as the responsibility to carry a job through to completion without having to continually go to those above them for an O.K. on even the smallest matter. . . . If top-level people are forced to conform to a lot of silly (to them) rules, they start to fight the company rather than work for it."

On the other hand, here are some reasons they gave for leaving previous employers:

"Too much and too detailed supervision. Supervisors were always pushing employees to work harder and faster; excessive overtime; much of the work was of a clerical nature."

"One-man show—past, present, and future. The over-all management philosophy was incompatible with my fundamental ideas and personal drives."

"Company appeared to be a one-man organization, i.e., no delegation of authority."

Pretty clearly, job attitudes will be constructive in direct relation to the freedom of individuals to act on their own. But organizational purpose cannot be achieved without discipline. Hence, freedom to act can't be given directly. It must grow out of the management system.

As our business organizations have grown in size, limitations on individual freedom have become a matter of national concern. As John Gardner says in *Self-Renewal:*

Every thoughtful man today worries about the novel and subtle restraints placed on the individual by modern large-scale organization. . . . A modern society is—and must be— characterized by complex organization. It is not a matter of choice. We must cope as best we can with the pressures that large-scale organization places on the individual.[2]

The best way, I believe, to cope with these pressures on the individual is to manage them by system. The right kind of system will enable capable (not necessarily brilliant) leaders of large-scale organizations to encourage the individual to act on his own—and, in so doing, still to carry out company strategy to achieve company objectives.

Opportunity to advance on merit: As we have seen, the opportunity to advance on merit (which implies that growth is a company objective) provides powerful executive motivation: more money, more prestige, more freedom to act on one's own. Here are some comments from participants in my high-talent survey that put this motive into perspective:

> "Advancement of the individual is the key to efficiency and success of the company. Therefore advancement should be based on solid factors, such as ability, capability and results— rather than on associations (even nepotism) and longevity. Politics are useful for external relations, but not for internal operations."

> "A good man leaves a company for two reasons, usually: a change and a raise. If these can be provided periodically at home—he will not leave."

> "I have become associated with a firm which is among the most outstanding in the industry. There are many opportunities to advance both in the States and in foreign offices."

> "Job advancement potential for high-talent men is enormous. Company is psychologically on threshold of accepting and using modern management techniques—which further enlarges job potentials."

Reasons given by the respondents for leaving previous employers included nepotism, inability to advance in a family business, too many good men waiting in line for advancement, and "civil service atmosphere"—in short, lack of opportunity to advance.

Sense of achievement: "The strongest motivating force in the human being, barring self-preservation, is *pride of achievement*." This statement was not made by a psychologist, philosopher, or academician—it was made by Ben D. Mills, vice president of the Ford Motor Company.[3]

Mr. Mills's view is borne out by my high-talent survey. Asked to indicate the reasons that most influenced them to remain with their present companies, 83 percent of the respondents checked the statement: "My work is interesting and challenging." Of those who had changed jobs, 53 percent cited lack of challenge as the reason, as against only 46 percent who left for more money.

From talking with hundreds of men whose job attitudes ranged from real dedication to active dissatisfaction, I know that a high-caliber man will rarely continue in work that lacks interest and challenge. In the wonderful American economy with its job mobility, the outstanding type of man that companies need for continuity of management just won't stay long in a dull, routine job that requires work he knows to be unimportant.

Many high-level executives I know rebel against this reality, decrying what they see as the unwillingness of young men today to settle down in their jobs. Those executives had better do more than bemoan the existence of the problem. If they don't, their companies will lose out in today's great talent hunt for the managers of tomorrow. Thirty-three percent of the respondents in my high-talent survey—all of them fairly young—reported that they had had jobs in two companies, 13 percent in three, and another 6 percent in four companies or more. Here are comments from a few of the men who had changed companies:

> "I was able to complete any assignments without having to operate at top speed or capacity. I changed to a bigger firm to work harder and consequently be offered greater compensation for a job well done."

> "The job did not require full utilization of my abilities, nor did it seem likely to in the future."

> "The first job was too routine, and looked like a slow, easy, secure job, but boring."

> "Work was frustrating; not all my aptitudes were being utilized."

> "Did not believe I was earning my salary, as I was unable to utilize my background and knowledge on the job."

David C. McClelland, a Harvard University psychologist, has done extensive research into achievement and achievers. In a *Harvard Business Review* article based on his book *The Achieving Society,* Professor McClelland reports that "it is *not* profit per se that makes the businessman tick but a strong desire for achievement, for doing a good job." [4] That, you'll recall, is the same conclusion the Swiss school principal reached after his U.S. visit.

The sense of achievement can be fully satisfied only when the evidence of achievement is clearly apparent to the man himself. A wise businessman once remarked to me that the outstanding executive wants "measures of his accomplishments that show him milestones of his achievements." Advancement and more money are two very tangible milestones; but praise and recognition are milestones too.

Clearly when the job provides little sense of achievement,

the capable man will leave it. And most of the capable men will leave despite the influence of pensions, bonus schemes, and stock options. This is fortunate for the economy, since it means that our great natural resource of executive manpower is finding the places where it can be most productive. But the moral is obvious for the individual managment that has the will to manage for company success. That is why I believe the management system should include a specific executive manpower strategy, designed to fit the company's executive needs and attitudes.

Rewards

Financial reward is such an obvious means of activation that I mention it only to put it in proper perspective. Many managements, in my opinion, tend to overrate what money can do to make a man productive in an executive job. Even if financial rewards in some form (salary, bonus, stock options, pension benefits, or other supplementary compensation) cause a man to stay with the company, they do not necessarily make him work productively.

Long observation and many confidential discussions have convinced me that, almost without exception, high-caliber men expect to be well paid and will leave if they aren't. They want the money not only for what it will buy but as recognition of performance and a milestone of achievement. When used in a system of management, the motivating force of financial reward will be increased by the interaction of managing processes and other job satisfactions.

Even though he knows he can get 20 percent more money somewhere else, the typical high-caliber man will stay and work productively in a well-managed business—provided his job offers him freedom to act on his own, opportunity to advance on merit, and a sense of achievement. (Perhaps 20 percent is even low.) Conversely, the financial reward must be disproportionately high to hold a high-caliber man in a poorly managed business or in a job where he is not free to act on his own, has limited opportunity to advance on merit, and/or little sense of achievement. Even if the higher financial reward does hold him, he will not work under such conditions as productively as he might.

At the time of his seventieth birthday in 1961, Sidney Weinberg of Goldman Sachs & Company, one of the most successful men on Wall Street, was interviewed by a *New York Herald Tribune* reporter. Asked whether he had a philosophy about money, Mr. Weinberg said, "Never work for money alone. Work for pride of achievement. If you work with this aim you'll make enough money to keep you. . . ." [5]

So financial reward should be kept in perspective. If it is used in gear with other motivators in the system, its effectiveness as an activator will be that much greater.

Other nonfinancial rewards, of course, also gain in motivational force when used as part of a system. Chief among these are group approval and disapproval. Then more money and job dismissal can be added as rewards and penalties. Mr. Mills of Ford is in agreement with Mr. Knudsen of GM when he says: "If the job is good, he gets the credit. If it is consistently bad, he should be replaced by a more competent man."

Commitment

Some years ago, a man in our commuting village gave up a job in a big New York City company to buy an automotive repair business. President, foreman, and the hardest worker of his small staff, he is already at work when the rest of us are boarding the morning train, and he is still at it when the trains bring us home at night. Yet he has nothing but sympathy for his friends who must commute to an office job in New York. With him, what began as interest ripened into commitment and flowered in dedication to his little business. His resulting success has enabled him to buy several other small businesses. He is a splendid example of the purposeful productivity of the individual proprietor to which I have already referred—a productivity that stems from interest, commitment, and dedication, in that order of intensity.

The person who is interested in his work is, of course, more productive than the one who does it just to earn a living. The person who is committed to his company and/or his work will be even more productive, because he begins to lose himself in his work—to find the work satisfying for itself, not just as a meal ticket. And the man who becomes dedicated to his company and/or his work begins to approximate the purposeful productivity of the lawyer in the large firm and the proprietor of the small business. He is the most productive of all.

The challenge to the large-scale enterprise is to stimulate the interest of its executives in their work and in the enterprise itself to the point where their performance will begin to match the productiveness, enthusiasm, and zest of the typical individual proprietor. Job interest, as we have seen, is essential even to hold the high-caliber man. But skillful and effective management can extend the interest of some to the stage of commitment and of a few to the stage of dedication.

The goal of commitment, even dedication, is *not* utopian. Countless executives throughout American business are *already* putting in unconscionable hours, making great personal and family sacrifices, and otherwise putting out well beyond the call of duty. What causes them to do this? And how can any top management create the conditions that will bring about a similar output of productive effort?

Such commitment or dedication can only be achieved in a

well-managed business which has a sound philosophy, offers a reasonable degree of individual freedom, provides opportunity for advancement on merit, and creates a sense of achievement. But even this is not enough; three further conditions must be met. The individual must believe in the worthwhileness of the work of the enterprise, he must have a sense of belonging, and he must understand the importance of his own work to the total accomplishments of the enterprise. Other conditions, such as respect and liking for his executive associates, will contribute to his commitment and dedication, but these are the essentials.

In a competitive economy only a slight edge in executive commitment or dedication can produce outstanding company success. In fact, commitment or dedication on the part of just a few executives is a sign that the company has created conditions that will make most of its other executives more productive. And this adds up to an enormous competitive advantage.

Worthwhileness of work: "It is essential that man's hunger for dedication be directed to worthy objects," John Gardner says in *Self-Renewal.* "The self-renewing man knows that if he has no great conviction about what he is doing he had better find something that he can have great conviction about. Obviously, all of us cannot spend all of our time pursuing our deepest convictions. But everyone, either in his career or as a part-time activity, should be doing something about which he cares deeply. And if he is to escape the prison of the self, it must be something not essentially egocentric in nature." [6]

In a speech about his forthcoming retirement as president of GM, made at the annual employees' Christmas program in 1964, John F. Gordon said: "I believe that you and I can be proud of our daily contributions to the society in which we live." As a dedicated executive himself, Mr. Gordon knew the importance to every high-caliber person of contributing to society, and he was doing his job as a leader in articulating that thought to employees and relating their work to it.

If business is to attract high-caliber men from the colleges and graduate schools—let alone develop them into productive executives—every business leader must somehow demonstrate that his company and others *do* contribute to society—that business does more than just make money. How can he accomplish this?

First, he should develop in his company the concept that profit, in a competitive economy, is a by-product of worthwhile effort. Since a product or service, no matter how mundane it may be, cannot continue to exist unless it does serve society, a realistic, tough-minded argument can be made for nearly every product. (Admittedly, the value set by the public on some products and services is so hard to fathom that it is difficult to see how those companies can even hope to attract high-caliber people.)

Second, he should use the strong and realistic argument that a successful business provides jobs. To be sure, this is a by-product of business activity. But there is growing recognition of the psychic importance of work for everyone.

Third, the high-caliber man can understand the importance to our society of favorable balances of trade and payments. The strength of the dollar is important not only to our own society, but to other nations throughout the world. And United States leadership of the West depends on the leadership of United States business.

Fourth, the high-caliber man can understand the importance of a successful business community in order to protect the United States and the entire free world from predatory international communism. United States industry must be able not only to create weapons for defense and resources for foreign aid, but also to keep the Communist world from burying us economically.

As a close observer of many businesses, I can easily appreciate the enormous contributions of business to society. But I believe that business itself must do a better job of identifying and articulating these contributions if it is to attract high-caliber people, and especially if any individual company is to develop the executive commitment and dedication that are needed to maximize its success. High-caliber men want to contribute significantly to society, but too many of them don't adequately recognize how a job in business—or a particular job in a particular company—enables them to do so.

Sense of belonging: Students of management, consulting psychologists to business, practical leaders of highly successful companies, and executives themselves all agree that high productivity, commitment, and dedication require a sense of belonging. In fact, the fundamental difference between a crowd of people and an organization of people is the shared objectives and shared beliefs of the people in the organization. How deeply they feel about the organization's objectives and beliefs and how much they share them determine their sense of belonging.

Consequently, top-management executives are learning that one of the best ways to develop a sense of belonging is to encourage people to participate in setting goals and objectives. That is one of the approaches Floyd Hall used in providing leadership for the turn-around of Eastern Air Lines. The capable executive gets his people to participate not only to keep them from feeling like cogs in a machine, but to increase their purposeful productivity.

In discussing his use of management by objectives, Ben Mills of Ford tells how he meets with department managers to discuss their objectives and goals. He says: "Of course, a clear *understanding* of the objectives in the mind of every individual is an absolute essential. It's impossible for anyone to identify himself with the accomplishment of the objective of the enterprise if he doesn't understand it. And if he has no personal identification with the objective, he has no basis for personal pride of achievement."

A second way to create a sense of belonging is through articulation of goals and their importance to the company. The new management of Eastern Air Lines did this through conferences, meetings, pamphlets, advertising—and even a $100,000 color motion picture.

Speaking at the University of Chicago, Frederick R. Kappel, chairman of AT & T, declared: "The very first requirement of top management is the ability to shape and state goals that will inspire men to strive toward them. To ask the right questions, to involve others in the search for the right answers, to create the targets and communicate what they are— these constitute the great challenge to business leadership. . . .

"You insist on their risk-taking, but you also share it with them. . . . You convey and you also learn, you impart and you listen, you communicate and you respond, and through this process you somehow get other people to share your purposes and work for them with you." [7]

And a respondent in my high-talent survey wrote that he had stayed with his company because "A most unusual atmosphere of 'belonging' and participating exists here. We are most fortunate in having attracted a very bright group of young, modern management men at all levels of operation." Another wrote: "Top company, fine personnel with excellent top management. Aggressive organization in a highly competitive industry, meeting the challenge of the times. Glad to be a part of the company." Another: "Very real feeling of belonging." And still another: "Top management knows who I am, where I am, and what I am doing."

Relationship of a person's work to company performance: Finally, to gain an executive's commitment and dedication to the company, it is important to give him an understanding of how his own work fits into that of the company, why his own job is important to company success. David H. Dawson, Du Pont executive committee member, puts it this way: "It is highly important, and increasingly so, to be sure that each individual can derive from his job a personal sense of satisfaction and a conviction that he is continuing to increase his contribution to the common effort." [8] Every man wants to know where *he* fits into the scheme of things.

Because he accepts the necessity for large-scale enterprises, the high-caliber man recognizes that, realistically, he must be something of a cog in the machine. But as a price for his commitment or dedication he demands the knowledge that the enterprise is doing worthwhile things, that he belongs, and that he is making an important contribution. The leadership of any enterprise that seeks to attract and retain high-caliber men is responsible for seeing to it that these and other demands of the high-caliber man are met.

Leadership

The best means of activating people, of course, is leadership. Leadership skill is needed in some depth by every company that aims to achieve maximum success.

Fortunately, the nature of business leadership and the tools required for developing it in depth are such that this need can more easily be met in a system-managed company. Such a company can be more successful with a given amount of leadership skill; and where the will to manage is present, a management system tends almost automatically to foster the development of that skill.

Extent of need: Since only a minor competitive advantage can enable a company to gain substantial success, business strategy need not be designed to achieve a towering competitive position like that of General Motors. Such competitive superiority is neither necessary nor common. Moreover, even GM built its present share-of-market from an initial position of slight competitive advantage which it compounded through systematized management.

The elements of business success are numerous, and many companies can be successful without leadership skill in great depth. But it is wise to aim high in developing leadership skill, since the more a company possesses, the greater its success is likely to be.

Although leadership is desirable at all levels in a company, it is most important in the chief executive and those reporting to him. In any company the number of key leaders required is not very great, and in a large company the proportion can be small indeed.

Nature of business leadership: When we think of "leadership" in the abstract, we are inclined to think of statesmen like a Lincoln or a Churchill—someone who can arouse or inspire men to rise to great achievements by perceiving their capacities and motivations, articulating the goals to be achieved, and inspiring the efforts and sacrifices needed to achieve them. In this sense, leadership seems somehow mystical—and unattainable for the ordinary person.

But I believe that *business* leadership—the only kind with

which we are dealing here—does not require vastly superior or unusual qualities, especially in a system-managed company. Given a chief executive with the will to manage, most system-managed companies can attract a reasonable proportion of high-caliber people and from them develop the leaders they need for success. It doesn't quite come about automatically, but it is fairly likely to happen if the system is followed.

I have two reasons for believing this. First, a system-managed business is not really dependent on personal leadership of an inspirational nature, desirable though such leadership always is. The various system components provide people in the business with guidelines for action. The individual's economic and emotional self-interest will cause him to follow these guidelines without a high order of inspired leadership. Since he knows what to do, self-government under the system will encourage him to do it. And the interactions of system components will further stimulate his performance.

Second, the requirements of business leadership are less demanding than those of great political leadership. The statesman must arouse people to do the unusual; the business leader need only stimulate them to do well in the task of earning their livelihood. Not that business may not demand sacrifice: I know one 47-year-old executive of a large company who has moved his family 28 times. But business sacrifices usually involve a larger and more perceptible element of self-interest than civic sacrifices. In fact, truly inspirational statesmanship moves citizens to put aside their self-interest. Business leadership, though it does appeal to people's higher motives, seldom has to meet such a challenge.

Next, a look at the qualities that business leaders need shows that men with those qualities are likely to be found in a system-managed company.

Every basic analysis of leadership emphasizes the importance of integrity. As Pearl S. Buck, the only American woman thus far to win the Nobel Prize for Literature, has said: "Integrity is honesty carried through the fibres of the being and the whole mind, into thought as well as action so that the person is complete in honesty. That kind of integrity I put above all else as an essential of leadership." [9] People won't follow a person they don't trust. But integrity is widely scattered in the population.

A business leader must have a good but not necessarily brilliant mind; reasonable degrees of imagination, initiative, and sustained drive; considerable achievement motivation; and some ability to understand the position and point of view of the other fellow. Again, these basic qualities are widely scattered in the population.

Thus, countless individuals possess all of the qualities required for effective business leadership. Yet, they lead poorly, if at all, because they don't know how to go about it. As executives with authority, they settle for orders and discipline. They fail to create constructive job attitudes. They lose for their companies the great potential advantages of self-direction and self-control.

Forces favoring the development of business leaders: Three primary forces at work in our society favor the development of leadership skill in U.S. business today:

1. *A free society:* Anyone in the United States can aspire to any level of business leadership for which he is fitted by his personal capabilities and ambition, just as he can aspire to leadership in government or any other field. Hence, a policy of advancement on the basis of performance is really useful in encouraging people to perform well and become leaders as well as managers.

2. *Universal education:* Our generally accepted *require-ment* for a high minimum level of education and the *opportunity* to get a graduate education that our society affords to any capable and ambitious person develop leadership skills for business as well as other fields.

3. *The free enterprise system:* The competitive profit-and-loss system is a great help to the leader at any level in a company. Fortunately, in the United States at least, most people still regard profit as the one measure of business success that is best for employees, stockholders, and citizens generally. Hence, business leadership is fostered simply by getting everyone in the company to recognize that long-term profit is the best single measure of company success and the most useful guide to decision making and action. In fact, the profit-and-loss system not only helps develop leadership skill but reduces the *need* for that skill by providing guidelines for self-direction and self-control.

Yet it is surprising how often business executives fail to make full use of this wonderful management and leadership tool. Many, for example, prefer to use volume, size, or prestige as measures of success. Many others simply fail to make effective use of the profit measure. It is a powerful and effective management and leadership instrument, and it is available to every business leader.

In addition to these general forces favoring the development of business leadership skill in the United States, a *system-managed* company has two additional advantages. A system of management (1) reduces the *need* for leadership and (2) provides specific assistance in *learning* leadership and making it effective in action.

How system reduces the need for leadership: In discussing leadership, Semon Knudsen of GM said that a leader "is a man with a mission." In a system-managed company the mission is clear because objectives and strategy are definite elements of management. Not only the top managers but executives at all levels have strategic plans before them. The mission does not depend on a single individual, because the system approach keeps many minds focused on the company's objectives and goals for increasing volume, share-of-market, and profits, and for maintaining continuity of effective management.

The same is true of the other managing processes. With all of the guidelines provided by the system, people know what to do and can get on with the job. The need for orders, penalties, and advice is minimized, and the company moves closer to the self-government end of the activating spectrum.

A system-managed business carries on a continuous hunt for talent and a continuous program for developing and motivating that talent. The better the talent, the less external activating it needs. With guidelines set by the system, self-direction and self-control are purposeful and productive.

Finally, by interaction the various managing processes that make up the system tend to support each other, thus reducing the need for leadership activation. For example, if the philosophy calls for decisions based on facts, managers at any level feel free to change their plans and programs as conditions change and new facts are disclosed. With established policies and clearly delegated authority, they can make decisions without waiting for either instructions or leadership from higher up.

Thus, action under one managing process interacts with actions under other processes within the system to strengthen all the actions and processes involved. Moreover, people lean more heavily on the *system* and less heavily on personal instructions, attitudes, and power. Once the system is established and understood by the people in the company, therefore, a system-managed company is actually easier to manage.

How the system helps develop leadership skill: Even though a system-managed company requires less leadership skill to achieve success, the system nevertheless helps to develop that skill. This is simply because the leader in a system-managed company knows better what to do to *be* a leader.

There is nothing mystical about the leadership process in a system-managed company. The leader at any level merely takes the steps necessary to build, articulate, support, and operate the system. These steps, in *themselves,* constitute adequate leadership for company success. Beyond this, whatever the leader accomplishes through brilliance in strategy, risk-taking, administration, or stimulation of people will be limited only by his own capabilities and ambitions. The system will give leverage to any brilliance he may possess. For a given input of ideas and actions, it will make him more productive. In short, it will increase his chances of becoming a Carnegie, Ford, Firestone, Sloan, or Watson.

In summary, then, here's how the system approach provides guidance and leverage for business leadership:

1. *The decision to systematize:* A decision by the head of any company, division, or department to systematize the business is in itself an act of leadership. Yet it is an easy, specific step to take—a concrete way of making the will to manage effective in achieving company success.

In deciding to systematize the business, the executive makes two commitments to himself: first, to maintain the will to manage; second, to devote much of his time to building, maintaining, articulating, and supporting the system and to making it effective in action. This means that he will have less time for day-to-day operational decision making. He will have to keep out of the details. He will be forced into a leadership posture.

2. *Company philosophy:* Crystallizing or shaping a company philosophy to control "the way we do things around here" is also an act of leadership, because it involves establishing a fact-founded approach to decision making and developing a greater sense of competitive urgency.

3. *Strategic and management planning:* Leadership by ideas that build volume and share-of-market can be supplied by requiring that concrete strategies and management plans are developed to provide specific answers to these questions: What kind of business should we be in? Why should customers buy our products or services? What problems need to be solved? What opportunities can we capitalize on?

Ideas are one of the few ways to gain a real competitive advantage, but the top-management executive need not furnish the ideas himself. He can stimulate the production of ideas from others by requiring them to develop alternative objectives and strategies and by insisting that they tackle any problems arising from shifts in external forces at work.

4. *Action guidelines:* Building the system requires the establishment of many action guidelines: a plan of organization, policies, standards, procedures, management plans, and information for managing. Certainly these guidelines are concrete ways of providing leadership. As they become known and used, they facilitate self-government.

5. *Personnel leadership:* The head of any organizational unit can provide important leadership by leading the talent hunt for high-caliber people. Then he can see to it that plans and programs are prepared for developing and motivating these people to become supervisors and executives qualified for advancement.

High-caliber people who know the company's philosophy,

who are qualified as executives, and who have been trained in the company's system can give any company a competitive advantage that is hard to duplicate. So, by devoting substantial time to this system component, the top executives provide leadership.

6. *System articulation:* As the system becomes established, it must be communicated—to executives and supervisors at a minimum, but preferably to everyone. The leader cannot do less than discuss the system orally with key executives to be sure they understand all the components and how they interact on one other. If it is to guide people, a system must be known and understood by the people to be guided—the more of them the better. Hence, the leader should put all the components of the system into writing—perhaps in the form of a pamphlet presenting the over-all system and its components, emphasizing their relative importance, and clearly describing their interaction.

But a general pronouncement is only the beginning of articulation. After that, every management communication, whether oral or written, should tie the specific action into the system. No orders, advice, discipline, reward, or other activating or motivating action should be taken unless it is tied clearly into the system. "Let's do this. Here is how it fits into the system and interacts with other components."

Once established, a system will not be useful or even hold together unless it is consciously used and believed in. The leader must constantly reiterate, in all his written and oral communications, what the system is, how it works, and why it helps to do the managing job. The will to manage through a system requires the will to build an effective system and the determination to articulate it constantly.

7. *System support:* The best way to kill a management sys-

tem is to violate it. The second best way is to ignore it. So the leader must support the system by following it himself and by inspiring and requiring others to do likewise.

Support and articulation go hand in hand. By following the system himself and explaining to others what is accomplished by doing so, the leader sets an example and so communicates in the most powerful way possible. And by training his subordinates to take the same approach, he can build a momentum for managing that both stimulates leadership and minimizes the need for leadership.

A superb expression of the value of the system approach to managing is found in a statement made at the 1965 meeting of General Motors stockholders by John F. Gordon, on the eve of his forthcoming retirement as president: "It has been GM's people—the individual and collective contributions of thousands of men and women down through the years—who have been responsible for the Corporation's consistently outstanding performance.

"Let me make it clear that I am not contending that General Motors men and women are inherently superior people. Individually, they probably cover as broad a range of capabilities as you will find in most large companies.

"It is what happens when you put them together that makes the difference. It is the potency of the mixture rather than the strength of its ingredients that is most important. General Motors is a very potent mixture of many different ingredients . . . its basic organization takes this wide diversity of elements fully into consideration. Its decentralized operations and responsibilities with centralized policies and coordinated control make it possible to balance . . . things like individual initiative and freedom of action on the one hand with guidance and restraint on the other.

"Working in such an organization, people not only act individually but react positively upon one another. Each person can and usually does increase the effectiveness of those with whom he works as well as his own effectiveness—and it makes their total performance considerably greater than the sum of their separate acts.

"Unexceptional men and women turned in exceptional performance for many reasons: for personal recognition, for monetary reward, for advancement and for personal satisfaction; also because of the urge to excel and to compete successfully, out of loyalty to the Corporation and to the people they work with—and for every possible combination of these and other motives."

8. *Constructive job attitudes:* Part of the down-the-line communication and training job is to give everyone a belief in the worthwhileness of the company's contribution to society, a sense of belonging and participation, and—at least at the supervisory level and up—an understanding of their contributions to the total enterprise. This is an intangible act of leadership, but again the system provides substantial assistance.

9. *Opportunities and problems:* An effective system of management will disclose opportunities that can be seized and problems that should be solved. If the system fails to produce the action indicated, the leader will have to step in. Especially should he see that personnel problems are dealt with promptly, fairly, and firmly.

10. *Dealing with extremes:* When the system functions poorly, as at times it will, the leader must be ready to act himself, choosing the activators and motivators most appropriate for the occasion. The system will still give leverage to his actions.

And even when the system is functioning well—as it should

be most of the time—the executive can add vision, zeal, inspiration, exhortation, or brilliance in any form or degree. If in so doing he does not interfere too much with the system, he will add to his company's success. But leadership in a system-managed company seldom requires such unusual abilities.

As you put down this book, I hope that your will to manage is strong. I hope, too, that you have come to share my conviction that a management system provides the best means for making that will to manage effective—the best way for your company to expand its volume and share-of-market, increase its long-term profits, and provide for continuity of effective management. Translated into action, that will and that conviction can bring substantial benefits to any enterprise. And enormous benefits for the nation will flow from the improvements in many enterprises.

Notes

Chapter 1

1. Alfred P. Sloan, Jr., *My Years with General Motors,* Doubleday & Company, Inc., New York, 1964, p. 4.
2. Frederic G. Donner, "The Development of an Overseas Operating Policy," McKinsey Foundation Lectures, Columbia University, April 28, 1966.

Chapter 2

1. Thomas J. Watson, Jr., *A Business and Its Beliefs,* McGraw-Hill Book Company, New York, 1963, pp. 5–6.
2. Alfred P. Sloan, Jr., *My Years with General Motors,* Doubleday & Company, Inc., New York, 1964, pp. xiii–xxiv.
3. Thomas C. Dillon, "Foot Dragging Made Easy," speech to the American Marketing Association, Dallas, Texas, June 16, 1964.
4. Charles E. Wilson, "Productivity—The Key to Prosperity and Peace," speech before the First Conference of Manufacturers, New York City, December 3, 1951.

Chapter 3

1. *Celanese World,* January, 1966.
2. Dean Acheson, "Ethics in International Relations Today," address at Amherst College, December 9, 1964.
3. From *The Living Lincoln,* edited by Paul M. Angle and Earl Schenck Miers, Rutgers University Press, New Brunswick, N.J., 1955.
4. Gerald L. Phillippe, "The Public Be Served," speech to the National Industrial Conference Board, October 29, 1964.
5. J. W. Keener, "Marketing's Job in the 1960s," *Journal of Marketing* (national quarterly publication of the American Marketing Association), January, 1960.
6. David R. Jones in *The New York Times,* September 7, 1964.
7. *The Wall Street Journal,* December 14, 1964, p. 1.
8. In a booklet entitled *This is Merrill Lynch, Pierce, Fenner & Smith, Inc.,* 1963.
9. In its report entitled "Technology and the American Economy" (1966).
10. From "The Mary Gloster" by Rudyard Kipling.

Chapter 4

1. George S. Dively, in a speech before the General Management Meeting of the American Management Association, May 20, 1959.
2. Richard R. Deupree, "Management's Responsibility toward Stabilized Employment," speech delivered at the Conference on General Management, American Management Association, October 11, 1945.
3. Robert McLean, "Ochs and Journalism: An Appraisal," *The New York Times Magazine,* March 9, 1958.
4. Stanley C. Allyn, "American Business Goes Abroad—A Case History," speech at Harvard Business School Conference, June 16, 1956, reprinted in *Harvard Business School Bulletin,* Summer 1956.
5. *Business Week,* September 21, 1957.
6. Robert R. Bowie, "Analysis of Our Policy Making Machine," *The New York Times Magazine,* March 9, 1958.

Chapter 5

1. Alfred P. Sloan, Jr., *My Years with General Motors,* Doubleday & Company, Inc., New York, 1964, p. 27.
2. Ralph Cordiner, "Problems of Management in a Large Decentralized Organization," speech to General Management Conference, American Management Association, June 19, 1952.
3. Exodus 18: 24–26.
4. *The New York Times,* June 16, 1961.
5. *The New York Times,* November 3, 1958.
6. *The New York Times,* May 15, 1964.

Chapter 6

1. *The New York World-Telegram* and other Scripps-Howard newspapers, August 29, 1956.
2. *The New York Times,* November 7, 1955.
3. Carnegie Corporation, *Annual Report for 1956.*
4. Published in *The Times,* London, May 25, 1956.
5. "The Great Talent Search: With Industry's Growing Complexity Comes Increased Need for Management Skills," *Du Pont Stockholder,* Winter, 1957–58.
6. See "Automation and the Middle Manager," report on a survey published by the American Foundation on Automation and Employment, Inc., 1966.
7. *The New York Times,* September 23, 1956.
8. John W. Gardner, *Self-Renewal: The Individual and the Innovative Society,* Harper & Row Publishers, Incorporated, New York, 1963, 1964, p. 11.
9. "Getting Ahead in General Motors," *Forbes,* December 1, 1962.
10. John W. Gardner, *Self-Renewal: The Individual and the Innovative Society,* Harper & Row Publishers, Incorporated, New York, 1963, 1964, p. 77.
11. *The New York Times,* January 29, 1965.

Chapter 7

1. *Celanese World,* January, 1966.
2. Frederick R. Kappel, "Vitality in a Business Enterprise," McKinsey Foundation Lectures, Columbia University, 1960.

Chapter 8

1. Semon E. Knudsen, "The Change Seekers," *Michigan Business Review,* November, 1964.
2. John W. Gardner, *Self-Renewal: The Individual and the Innovative Society,* Harper & Row Publishers, Incorporated, New York, 1963, 1964, p. 55.
3. Ben D. Mills, "Management without Meddling," *Think* (IBM), October, 1958.
4. David C. McClelland, "Business Drive and National Achievement," *Harvard Business Review,* July/August, 1962.
5. *The New York Herald Tribune,* October 13, 1961.
6. John W. Gardner, *Self-Renewal: The Individual and the Innovative Society,* Harper & Row Publishers, Incorporated, New York, 1963, 1964, p. 99 and pp. 16–17.
7. Frederick R. Kappel, "Management, Computers, and Learning Power," presented at Thirteenth Annual Management Conference of the Executive Program Club and the Graduate School of Business of the University of Chicago, March 17, 1965.
8. D. H. Dawson, "Management Techniques and Personnel Development," presented at Symposium on Development of Chemical Management, Division of Industrial and Engineering Chemistry, American Chemical Society, Boston, Massachusetts, April 9, 1959.
9. Pearl S. Buck, "Principles of Leadership," Second Annual Gandhi Memorial Lecture at Howard University, Washington, D. C. (printed in *The American Review,* October, 1961).

Bibliography for the System-Builder

I have selected these few books as aids to any reader interested in developing a system of management for his company or division, improving some of its managing processes, or simply sharpening and deepening his own management perspectives. I believe they will help him to *think through* how the managing processes work—and how they can be fitted into a system of programmed management tailor-made for his particular company, division, or department.

These books will carry the reader deep into the literature of management, because most of them have references and bibliographies of their own. Many will have to be *studied,* not just *read,* since in choosing them I have been guided more by substance than by readability. I assume that any reader who has the will to manage also has the will to wade through a few texts and to browse in others.

Managing and Managing Processes

Dale, Ernest: *Management: Theory and Practice,* McGraw-Hill Book Company, New York, 1965.

> This broad and basic book about the whole field of management provides the system-builder with a useful background text. Contains selected readings, references, and a glossary of management terms.

Drucker, Peter F.: *Managing for Results: Economic Tasks and Risk-taking Decisions,* Harper & Row Publishers, Incorporated, New York, 1964.

Although it deals with fundamentals of management, the primary emphasis of this book is on entrepreneurial decision making designed to make the organization grow and prosper. I found three chapters particularly stimulating: Chapter 6, "The Customer Is the Business"; Chapter 7, "Knowledge Is the Business"; and Chapter 8, "This Is Our Business."

Fox, William McNair: *The Management Process: An Integrated Functional Approach,* Richard D. Irwin, Inc., Homewood, Illinois, 1963.

This is a management text covering the usual subjects, but valuable in the way it points up the interaction of the managing processes. An appendix contains a statement of basic management principles.

Newman, William H., and James P. Logan: *Business Policies and Central Management,* 5th ed., South-Western Publishing Company, Cincinnati, Ohio, 1965.

This is essentially a college and graduate-school textbook on management, by a leading professor at Columbia University's Graduate School of Business and a colleague. The table of contents, heading structure, and index will enable you to refer to the various system components; and the bibliography will help you to go deeper. The fundamental character and simplicity of the book make it a useful all-purpose tool for the system-builder.

Company Philosophy

Mortimer, Charles G.: *The Purposeful Pursuit of Profits and Growth in Business,* McGraw-Hill Book Company, New York, 1965.

These lectures by the then chief executive of General Foods Corporation outline a philosophy that has had a profound effect on that leading company's outstanding record of profitable growth.

Watson, Thomas J., Jr.: *A Business and Its Beliefs: The Ideas That Helped Build IBM,* McGraw-Hill Book Company, New York, 1963.

This brief and readable book shows how concepts and philosophy have contributed to the growth of a great corporation.

Strategic Plannning

Ansoff, H. Igor: *Corporate Strategy: An Analytic Approach to Business Policy for Growth and Expansion,* McGraw-Hill Book Company, New York, 1965.

This excellent treatment of objectives and strategy also presents problem-solving tools and techniques that will help a company reformulate its strategy. The author—a professor at the Graduate School of Industrial Administration of Carnegie Institute of Technology—combines fresh and imaginative thinking with his prior corporate planning experience in industry.

Learned, Edmund P., C. Roland Christensen, Kenneth R. Andrews, and William D. Guth: *Business Policy: Text and Cases,* Richard D. Irwin, Inc., Homewood, Illinois, 1965.

Don't be frightened by the bulk of this tome, written by three distinguished professors and an assistant professor at Harvard Business School, primarily for classroom use. Nestled among the cases (which can be skipped) are useful discussions of corporate strategy. Just use the table of contents to pick out perceptive and readable nuggets, none of which is very long.

Steiner, George A. (ed.): *Management Long-Range Planning,* McGraw-Hill Book Company, New York, 1963.

Report on a seminar of strategic (long-range) planners from leading corporations. Chapters 1 and 2 together cover only 79 readable pages, and give the best brief over-all view of the field I have found. Subsequent chapters describe in detail how various organizations do their long-range planning.

Organization Planning

Chandler, Alfred D., Jr.: *Strategy and Structure: Chapters in the History of the Industrial Enterprise,* The M. I. T. Press, Cambridge, Massachusetts, 1962.

This is a solid research study dealing in detail with the structure of four large corporations: Du Pont, General Motors, Jersey, and Sears. I suggest you read the conclusion and then decide, with the aid of the detailed table of contents, how deeply you want to dig into the rest of the book.

Learned, Edmund P., and Audrey T. Sproat: *Organization Theory and Policy: Notes for Analysis,* Richard D. Irwin, Inc., Homewood, Illinois, 1966.

This brief paperback—written by one of the distinguished Harvard Business School professors referred to earlier and a research associate at that school—provides an excellent lead-in to the study of organization. Actually it is an annotated bibliography, with comments about the books that will enable you to judge their usefulness in building your system.

Management Information and Control

Anthony, Robert N.: *Planning and Control Systems: A Framework for Analysis,* Division of Research, Graduate School of Business Administration, Harvard University, Boston, 1965.

In a little over 100 pages, the author does much more than develop a "framework for analysis"—he provides valuable and stimulating background that will be useful in developing the planning and control components of a management system. Dr. Anthony, a distinguished researcher and teacher now on leave from his post as Ross Graham Walker Professor of Management Controls at Harvard Business School, is currently making a practical application of his knowledge to a critical area of government as Assistant Secretary of Defense.

Anthony, Robert N., John Dearden, and Richard F. Vancil: *Management Control Systems: Cases and Readings,* Richard D. Irwin, Inc., Homewood, Illinois, 1965.

A combination text and case book by Dr. Anthony and two Harvard Business School colleagues. Excellent text material begins each chapter; the cases can be skipped. Use the table of contents to pick out "readings" on management information for control purposes.

Likert, Rensis: *New Patterns of Management,* McGraw-Hill Book Company, New York, 1961.

This outstanding (but not outstandingly readable) book contains several useful chapters on measurement and also covers other aspects of management creatively. An extensive bibliography is provided.

Neuschel, Richard F.: *Management by System,* McGraw-Hill Book Company, New York, 1960.

This is the second edition of *Streamlining Business Procedures,* a fundamental treatment of business systems and procedures by a colleague of mine. The system-builder can profit from the approach he outlines for keeping procedures and paperwork simple and low-cost.

Computers and Operations Research

Ackoff, Russell L., and Patrick Rivett: *A Manager's Guide to Operations Research,* John Wiley & Sons, Inc., New York, 1963.

An excellent introduction. The title is accurate, and the text is both readable and brief.

Solomon, Irving I., and Lawrence O. Weingart: *Management Uses of the Computer,* Harper & Row Publishers, Incorporated, New York, 1966.

This book will give the general executive a good start toward sophistication in a crucially important and fast-moving field.

Motivation and Leadership

Bennis, Warren G., and Edgar H. Schein (eds.): *Leadership and Motivation: Essays of Douglas McGregor,* The M. I. T. Press, Cambridge, Massachusetts, 1966.

A convenient selection of writings in which the system-builder can profitably browse for ideas on the development and activation of people.

McGregor, Douglas: *The Human Side of Enterprise,* McGraw-Hill Book Company, New York, 1960.

This stimulating and broad-ranging book deals with self-control in business and several other aspects of executive motivation and leadership.

Odiorne, George S.: *Management by Objectives: A System of Managerial Leadership,* Pitman Publishing Corporation, New York, 1965.

This brief book contains much of broad value to the system-builder. Several chapters deal in an especially searching way with executive motivation.

Patton, Arch: *Men, Money, and Motivation,* McGraw-Hill Book Company, New York, 1961.
This readable book treats the subjects in the title in a thoughtful and practical manner. The author, one of my colleagues, is a leading authority on executive compensation.

Zaleznik, Abraham: *Human Dilemmas of Leadership,* Harper & Row Publishers, Incorporated, New York, 1966.
This unusual book probes the inner psychology of the leader and explores the development and conflict of individuals in the organization setting. The treatment of personal power shows the value of a management system for controlling it.

INDEX

The Will to Manage

274

Dively, George S., *quoted*, 100–101, 116–117
Donner, Frederic G., *quoted*, 19
Douglas-Home, Sir Alec, *quoted*, 228–229
"Dragnet," 27
du Pont de Nemours, E. I., & Company, 55, 63, 67, 90, 95, 139, 150, 164, 178, 181, 183, 200, 229, 250
Durant, William C., 2–3, 7, 121

Eastern Air Lines, Incorporated, 20–21, 248
Economist, The, 76
Edison, Thomas, 225
Estes, Elliot M., *quoted*, 181
Ethical standards, 24–27
Ethyl Corporation, 86
Evaluation, performance (*see* Performance evaluation)
Ewald, John A., 26
Executive personnel administration, advancement and separation, 182–188
as system component, 156–158
Executive planning and development, 92–94, 158–161, 171–182
Executive recruitment, 161–171
Executive talent, 25, 63–64, 92–94, 113–114, 120–121, 126, 156–171, 183–184
(*See also* Executive personnel administration; Executive planning and development; Executive recruitment)

Fact-founded approach, 24, 27–33, 57, 109, 136, 138–139, 144, 176, 237
Federated Department Stores, Inc., 181
Fifty-fifty corporation, 85–87
Firestone, Harvey S., 256
First National City Bank of New York, 34–35
FMC Corporation, 78–80
Forces at work, 22, 24, 33–35, 43, 61
Ford, Henry, 256
Ford Motor Company, 241, 244, 249
Forecasting, 53–54
Foreign operations (*see* Overseas business)
Fortune magazine, *quoted*, 26
Friday, hero of "Dragnet," 27, 32
Functional authority (*see* Authority)

Gardner, John W., *quoted*, 162, 173, 182, 239–240, 246
General Electric Company, 62, 81, 82, 122, 150
General Foods Corporation, 68–69, 145–146, 181
General Motors Corporation, 2–3, 19, 28–30, 38, 68, 69, 71, 81, 83–84, 86, 121–122, 150, 176, 181, 218, 236, 244, 246–247, 251, 254–255, 259

Gillette Company, 43, 66, 145–146
Goals, corporate, 17, 64, 200–204
Goldman, Sachs & Co., 244
Goodrich, B. F., Company, 65
Gordon, John F., *quoted*, 246–247, 259–260
Great Atlantic & Pacific Tea Company, Inc., 98–100, 102, 109
Greeley, Horace, 54
Greenewalt, Crawford, 230
quoted, 229
Growth, company, 63–64

Hall, Floyd, 21, 248
Harris-Intertype Corporation, 100–101, 116–117
Harvard Business Review, 158, 242
Harvard Business School, 55, 107, 165
Harvard Business School Club of New York, 155
Harvard University, 242
Hemingway, Ernest, 225
Heyworth, Lord, *quoted*, 163–164, 174–175
Hicklin, Wayne, 26
High-caliber men (*see* Executive talent)
High-talent manpower, survey of, 158, 180, 183, 184, 238–242, 249–250
Hudson Motor Car Company, 71

Imperial Chemical Industries Ltd., 86
Industrial Copartnership Association, 37
Information systems, management, 216–222
International Business Machines Corporation, 23–24, 63, 85, 91, 92, 95
International operations (*see* Overseas business)
Investment Bankers Association, 2

Job attitudes, constructive, 237–243
Job rotation, 181–182
John Bean Manufacturing Co., 78
Johnson, President Lyndon B., 101
quoted, 80, 187
Johnson & Johnson, 68–69

Kappel, Frederick R., 55
quoted, 201, 249
Katzenbach, Nicholas, 183
Keener, J. W., *quoted*, 65, 68
Kipling, Rudyard, *quoted*, 96
Knorr, Fred, 156
Knudsen, Semon E., 244
quoted, 236, 238, 254–255

Leadership, 250–261
Leness, George J., 75